A Woman's Search for Serenity

Martha Nelson

BROADMAN PRESS
Nashville, Tennessee

C.L.

© Copyright 1972 • Broadman Press
All rights reserved
ISBN: 0–8054–5214–1
4252–14

248.8
Nel

The author is indebted to many for quotations which appear in this book. Acknowl-
edgements appear on pages 139–140.

Library of Congress Catalog Card Number: 78–178063
Dewey Decimal Classification: 248.8
Printed in the United States of America

*To my mother
and
our daughters,
Pat, Nancy, and Becky*

Preface

Serenity is not the kind of subject we women discuss when we get together. But we go on at length, in wildly descriptive terms, about its antithesis. . . .

"You wouldn't *believe* this morning!" we gasp, arriving late for our appointment.

"Jim's job is shaky," we confide with dark looks, and with fear in our voices, "I don't know what's happening to our Linda . . . she's not the girl she used to be."

"I'll go stir crazy if I have to look at these four walls much longer!"

And, threateningly, "If another thing goes wrong. . . ."

Serenity is an elusive quality these days. Technology has so drastically affected our way of life, and we have not readily adjusted. Dissonant voices about "woman's role" have added to our uncertainties. Daily we are faced with a clutter of complex choices.

And so—the search for serenity. There's challenge and excitement in such a search. Time is required for a thorough exploration, and sometimes the going is tough. But I hope you will find it, as I have, a personally rewarding adventure.

I am grateful to all whose lives and wisdom have enriched my thinking. I want to thank Dr. Charles P. Carlson, Chaplain Jack

Slaughter, and Jim Groen for their assistance; Mary Ann Hamilton, Mary Farmer, and Booncy Fullam for permission to use their stories; Tera Ray, Sue Hottle, and Gladys Lyth for their practical suggestions; and countless others who indicated areas of concern among women and shared their ideas with me.

Special thanks go to Joan Ambrosic, whose craftsmanship as a writer and insight as a Christian woman made her critique particularly valuable, and to Broadman editor Dr. William J. Fallis, who evaluated and made wise comment on each chapter. I am also grateful to Elsie Dozier for typing the manuscript.

Most of all, I am deeply grateful to my husband Carl whose concern for my relationship with God started me on my search many years ago and who has given loving guidance along the way. Many of the suggestions in the book have come from his extensive knowledge of the Word and his wealth of experience in counseling.

MARTHA NELSON

Littleton, Colorado
December 31, 1971

Contents

‖
Living Through a Major Move

". . . leaving? It sounds so easy!"
—Golde in *Fiddler on the Roof*

NO! I wanted to shout. I don't want to go!

Do we have to become a statistic—another of the one out of five American families to move this year?

Why do *we* have to be uprooted? I don't transplant very well. It takes so long for my roots to take hold.

I was content. I loved my fireside. With candles glowing, and people in, my home was lovely to my eye.

My husband's position was a continuing challenge, our income comfortable enough. No need to leave. The new work would be hard, and he wasn't getting any younger.

And the children! Becka, a high-school senior all set for a part in the annual spring musical. Nancy, her wedding announced for June, to be performed in our lovely church in the presence of longtime friends.

My job! "Not now!" I felt like crying out. "I've just been promoted, remember?"

I wasn't ready for a move. There was the terrace we had begun but not quite finished. The roses set out only last spring; the plants brought from my mother's yard; our dogwood—a promise of pure beauty just weeks away. And, under the hard-frozen ground, crocuses and tulips planted last fall pushing their way to light. The tulip package had promised, "Just put 'em in the ground and walk away whistling," and I had believed.

I thought of others in our community—the other four. The Warrens, living in the very house where Jim Warren had grown up as a boy, surrounded by the choicest of the familiar furnishings of his boyhood, with lilacs that had bloomed for his mother now blooming for his wife. The Allens, veritable pillars of church and community. The Burnetts, with married children living in the city, coming and going for suppers and family gatherings at will. The Marlars across the street, able to look in on their aging parents several times a week.

I liked that kind of security—of belonging, of knowing and of being known. . . .

Some of you will understand.

Women like Mildred, who, after thirty-eight years in a pleasant Oklahoma town, dug up her roots and left twin grandbabies behind to move west with her husband.

And like Gladys, who for the first time in her life had chosen the colors for each room in her house and had planted every blade of grass around it—and who cried all the way from Mississippi to Wyoming.

Ministers' wives like Anne, who lavished her love on the people of a church, only to have to tear herself completely away from them.

Women like Vera, who spent seven years in building and furnishing the home of her dreams, only to have her husband receive that promotion that couldn't be turned down. "When the company says, 'Will you?,' what can you do?"

Not all are like Betsy, traipsing from sunny, warm Orlando to Boston, with three dogs (one expecting) and her prize philodendron towed along in the family's second car. Betsy thoroughly enjoys a move: "It's a reason to clean the garage, to tackle the attic, to throw out a lot of junk. I love making new friends . . . have always wanted to see the world, and Boston's so historic. It gives me the feeling of a fresh start with life."

Or Millie and Jean, driving from West Texas to Butte, Montana, with six children, peanut-butter sandwiches, and a parakeet, in pouring rain, with luggage slipping around topside the station wagon: "When your guy's in construction, what's a woman to do?"

A few enjoy a move, but most of us admit we *don't* particularly look forward to one.

With that familiar one-in-five statistic glaring at us, we may as well be prepared emotionally—for it can happen. Not only do ministers' wives and military wives have to face the prospect of frequent moves, but it's a fact of life for executives' wives. Corporations move their men like checkers on a checkerboard—on an average of five times by age forty for rising young executives. In some companies a man must earn "service stripes" for five or six moves before he is permitted to establish a permanent home.

One moving firm declares it has helped some corporation families relocate more than ten times, and, according to Ninki Hart Burger, in *The Executive's Wife,* at least one veteran of the multi-move has had it: "If I ever again open my door and see the idiotically happy face of a Welcome Wagon representative, so help me, I'll grab her bundle of goodies and pelt her with them."

But the command to get up and go comes from Uncle Sam, if you're military; or from the man behind the mahogany desk, if you're corporation; or from the bishop, or a beckoning church, if you're a minister's wife. Oil has a way of playing out, and when houses and bridges are finished, construction men move on. And American women know they can't say no!

If there is a choice, it is one to be decided by a partnership, usually—you and your husband. And since it is a job-oriented decision (*his* job), you acquiesce to his deciding vote.

The choice is not always based on what is actually best for all concerned. Some corporations have begun to see that the decision to move should be made by company, husband and wife, and family. But others, blind to the two worlds in which every married man lives, still insist upon an unbending loyalty to the organization. Husbands and wives often find it difficult to evaluate the alternatives, if there are any. The drive to make it big is a part of the American lifestyle, and the promise of prestige and buying power tend to color the grass a little greener in distant cities.

A move, even a temporary dislocation, can be upsetting. Take Doug and Karen, our less-than-a-year-old grandchildren, transported halfway across the continent. Oh, yes, we were ready for them, with borrowed cribs, rocking chairs just waiting for babies to rock, and so much love begging to be shared. But, away from accustomed surroundings, where the household sounds were different, the temperature and lighting not quite the same, and so many strange people about, Doug and Karen had trouble adjusting. And especially in the evening! (Afterward our kindly next-door neighbors declared they had enjoyed hearing a baby cry again).

And there was Amy, nicely settled after six weeks in first grade, when her family moved. "I hate school," she would protest as her parents tried to push her along to school each morning. It was serious, until her father came up with the bright idea of providing her with a big sack of candies for sharing at recess.

There is Joey, in junior high. His dad has been transferred five times since Joey can remember. Every time he has had to give up some very special friend, and once, a dog he loved. Joey feels unsettled and he is reluctant to make friends. He can't say why, but the truth of the matter is Joey's been hurt so many times he's afraid to get deeply involved with anyone again. "Moving is hard on kids," one expert who works with youth said. "One emotionally disturbed girl with whom I counseled has moved thirteen times in her brief lifetime, and she doesn't know why she's disturbed. Kids are not always anxious to build lasting friendships only to have them broken. They begin to build up a psychological protection against others, against openness, even with adults who want to be helpful."

There is Kathy, away at college in a crowded freshman dorm —Kathy, who couldn't *wait* to get out from under the stifling supervision of Mother and Dad, now miserably, miserably homesick in her new environment.

There are elderly people, moved from their homes by urban renewal.

"If those were slums, I loved them," one of them said to a newspaper reporter.

Others commented,

"When people are old, you can't say these things to them—you've got to move, get out. They'll have a stroke or heart attack or something."

"It's not good when you want to be in one place and you have to go to another place to live."

"I can't believe it's worth all the heartache. It's hard to move into a new neighborhood. Although I like it here, I miss the old neighborhood. There, you were concerned . . . not in a nosey way. Here, I feel so helpless."

And there's you and you and you, and me.

How can a Christian woman cope with the problems involved in a move?

Start packing, you say? Agreed, it's a nasty job, the sooner finished, the better.

But wait—not just yet!

For transplanting a family is a lot like transplanting a flower or shrub, and careful handling pays off in the long run.

Now, some plants will survive if they are jerked up and transplanted, but gardeners who know and really care begin with preparation. A gardening book tells us: "The following instructions on how to plant shrubs and trees may seem a bit fussy. We know that there are quicker and easier ways to plant. But we assume that to be sure of success you are willing to spend a little more time and effort in planting and after-care than most people feel is necessary."

So, lesson number one: Plan on spending time and effort in making your transition. An oil company wife told me: "When we knew we were making a move, we spent a great deal of time preparing the children. (In fact, I was usually so busy boosting the children's morale that I didn't have time to get depressed.) Youngsters can learn very early that "this is how Daddy makes a living" and that moving is a part of it. When it's a promotion, I set the family climate with, "How proud we are of Daddy!" We get down the encyclopedia and atlas and begin looking for facts about our new location and soon we are planning next year's vacation and the Saturday trips we'll take.

"My mother's positive attitude has been a tremendous help. Mother thinks 'it's wonderful' wherever we are headed. She can't wait to come see us. In fact, she's dying for us to move to Alaska! Our children have been the envy of kids who have never known the delicious anticipation of a visit from their grandparents.

"I always try to point out the good in a new situation, to build into the children the idea that this year is better than the last. My efforts at optimism for their sake have kept me smiling, even in Casper, Wyoming.

"I've found it helps not to get too attached to a house. After all, it's a matter of value judgment. It's the people in a house that are important; the house is a mere thing."

The gardening experts tell us to dig well around the plant that's being moved. Don't disturb the roots any more than is absolutely necessary.

Lesson number two: Pack carefully. When you start sorting your belongings into piles of what to take and what to discard, be careful (one woman with a weakness for shoes decided to discard a few pair—somehow the good ones were thrown out and the movers picked up the discards). Of course, after a few hours you'll begin to feel like the man who took a job sorting potatoes and promptly resigned because it involved so many decisions. But don't get careless now! For how and what you pack will make a difference in how rapidly you and your family will likely adjust to a new house. The often small, most beloved family treasures can make a place into a home more quickly than anything else—a painting you love, a pottery pitcher, a quaint woven stool, a lamp or basket or candy jar, certain favorite books. It's the familiar that is hard to leave, and it is the familiar that can give an air of homeyness to the strange, faraway spot to which your family is transported.

By all means, pack a sense of humor where you can lay your hands upon it immediately. Mrs. Burger says it's absolutely essential if you're moving abroad, for life overseas becomes "a matter of leaning on laughter or grimly subsisting on a diet of small disasters." And it comes in handy in stateside moves as well.

Even the gardener who is not yet beyond the half-a-dozen tomato plants stage has learned to expect a wilt when she transplants. She shades her plants carefully, covers them against the unexpectedly cold evening, waters them faithfully, and watches over them daily. Knowing that the first few days of her ownership are the most critical days in the life of the plants, she gives them extra attention and tender, loving care. And usually, they begin to straighten up and then to grow.

Lesson number three for a woman on the move: Expect a time of grieving, of wilting if you please. Any time there is the loss of anything that is significant to you, a time of grieving follows. In the case of a move that picks you up and sets you down at a distance from old friends and family, away from the beloved surroundings you have called by that beautiful word "home," there comes a sense of sadness, of inexplicable loneliness, that only time can cure. As one in mourning, you find yourself remembering with nostalgia the things and people left behind. These more-often-than-not imperfect things and persons take on an aura of near-perfection as unpleasant memories slip away into your subconscious, leaving only what is pleasurable to recall. So don't despair. Give yourself and your family time to get over the loss you are experiencing. Allow a full season, at least, for your roots to take hold, and hang on to the assurance that they *will,* eventually. Allow time for lots of tender, thoughtful, loving care for the family during the transition period. A child just arrived home from a day in a strange school can be reassured with cookies and milk and a chance to talk things over. A displaced teen-ager may find a new friend in his parents in the interim between leaving old friends and making new ones. Husband, too, may thrive better with an extra portion of wifely encouragement and understanding during the settling-in days on his job.

The green-thumb gardener starts cultivating, once the roots of her plant begin to take hold. She's more careful about watering a recently transplanted plant and she may apply a special plant food from time to time.

Lesson number four: Once you're settled, begin cultivation. Feed the family with local information; cultivate a spirit of excitement and interest about new people and places; pack a lunch and drive off in a different direction on your days off. If there are neither mountains, nor lake, nor seashore, one veteran suggests that you try counting the varieties of wild flowers in a field.

One mobile wife said: "It was the people who sat around and did nothing who did the most griping when we were in Guam. The rest of us determined to make the best of the situation. We got out and looked for beauty, and you know, we especially saw the beauty of the natives there."

Get around and see the town. Find the library. And, of course, a church—for here the Christian family is likely to find a ready reception, as warm-hearted Christians reach out in friendship to those who come their way. Don't limit yourself to worship services: find your way into at least one of the small-group fellowships (Sunday School, training groups, missions organizations, choirs) where nodding acquaintances become people with similar problems and needs. Pitch in and do something, and find among your co-workers friends like you have left behind.

The gardener who learns how to prune has power at her fingertips, for with pruning she can direct growth, renew growth, produce more flowers. She never prunes just to be pruning, but always with the good of the plant in mind.

Lesson number five: Soon after a family transplant, consider pruning. A young woman moving from California to Minneapolis declared: "I love the first months after a move. The phone is quiet, I'm uninvolved with this and that for a change, and I have time to enjoy my children—to read to them and tea-party and walk in the park. It's 'lemonade,' for a while," she smiled. Many a family finding themselves overinvolved with oftentimes meaningless activities lack the quantities of courage required to bow out. A routine of expensive, time-consuming, often dull entertaining may be taking parents from children. Youngsters may belong to so many organizations they don't have time to relax. The wife may have continued working when she really prefers staying home. The standard of living may have begun to get out of hand. For some families a move offers opportunity for some much-needed pruning.

Too many Christian families, however, prune too heavily, ruthlessly chopping off relationships to other Christians. Eventually, if not immediately, the family suffers. "We were too involved," they often say, excusing their failure to unite with a church in another city or neighborhood. "We thought we'd rest awhile."

Rest awhile from worship, Bible study, sharing, and service? When there are children growing away from the teachings of the Word, growing away from a desire to worship, growing toward a religion of materialism and godlessness, what a sad decision! When trouble strikes, and there are no Christian friends in the community to give prayer support and to stand beside you, what a sad decision!

Can the Christian woman cope with a family transplant? Yes, if her concept of marriage is founded on the Christian ideal—that the two shall be one, that the husband is the head of the wife. And if her love makes her esteem her husband better than herself. If she is determined to do her part in making life enjoyable wherever his job takes him. If she interprets "for better for worse" to include the best and the worst of places where she may have to make a home. The unhappy woman who has followed her husband to some drab spot where he likes his work and is content might gain a new perspective if she could hear Judy describing how *her* husband hates his work and the unhappiness this is creating for her little family.

Only one in a million can live like Reneé, the young German girl who told me how she came to live in Denver. Her husband, just discharged from the army, looked around for work in Wisconsin where he had been stationed, and finding none, was forced to move on. "No special place in mind," she said, "we drove across the midwest, looking for a place to settle. When we drove into Denver, with its myriad of lights twinkling beneath us, we knew we had arrived. This is it! This is it!" we agreed. "He found work and a college to attend, I got a job, and here we are. We love it!"

But more often the city which has claimed the family on the move seems a bit forbidding as one wearily arrives on the scene.

The first nights and days, maybe even weeks, may be spent in a motel or an apartment, with your furniture enroute or in storage. You are faced with decisions about finding a house to buy, your kind of house, at your kind of price, in your kind of neighborhood. All the while you may be hurting from the loss you've had to take on the property you've left or worrying about the for sale sign still standing in the front yard. Then there are all of the details to be cared for—insurances, licenses, et cetera, et cetera, ad infinitum.

You don't know where to shop. You've no idea which doctor to call in an emergency. The budget is shaky. And, when you decide on a house, there's work to be done! Unpacking, purchasing, altering, rearranging, locating this and that—and you're tired. You look around and see the bare spots your furniture won't cover, and you look at the budget that can't stand the strain of new purchases right now. Or you step over the pieces the place just won't hold. You move the lamp or mirror that was perfect in your last house and here doesn't fit anywhere, and you could cry.

And Junior hates his teacher and Susie hasn't made any friends and Jim is lying awake nights worrying about the adjustments he must make at work.

The loneliness sets in. You may have been uprooted not only from a house, but from parents and other favorite relatives as well. You may have been uprooted, as I was, from a job you enjoyed and will have difficulty duplicating in your new city. . . .

"A good gardener," says Herb Gundell, the Rocky Mountain empire's most widely known authority on gardening, "takes one step at a time." He goes on to identify the steps, like digging five dollar holes for one dollar plants, carefully watering, protecting from cold and so on. And then he adds, "And finally, he accepts the dictates of our unusual mile high climate gracefully, without losing his desire or his nerve."

Lesson number six: The mobile woman accepts the unusual—be it climate, housing, neighborhood, or whatever—gracefully, with determination and, if need be, nerve!

The Christian woman can cope!

. . . like Sarah, who probably never complained when Abraham said, "We're packing and moving tomorrow, dear, and I'm not sure where we're heading yet."

. . . and like Ruth, who, widowed and lonely, said in those famous words to her mother-in-law: "Whither thou goest, I will go, and where thou lodgest I will lodge; thy people shall be my people, and thy god my god."

. . . and like me, who, knowing all the time I'd go, wanted to shout no to the idea of leaving behind my accumulation of friends and memories and achievements in Missouri, but who looked up at the glistening Gateway Arch, St. Louis' proud symbol of America's westward movement, and saw in a vision women in sunbonnets, packing their things into covered wagons.

We women have always gone with our men! We have followed them to their new frontiers. We've struggled alongside them in clearing and carving out a new place under the sun.

For home is wherever we're together, and we dare them to try to leave us behind!

2

Life Doesn't Have to Be So Hectic!

As soon as the rush is over
I'm going to have a nervous breakdown.
I worked for it, I owe it to myself
And nobody is going to deprive me of it.

Who hasn't wished at some point in life for just a few days with a "QUIET PLEASE" sign dangling from the doorknob!

But nervous breakdowns are no longer stylish, and today's woman is hard-pressed to find an escape.

Serenity? When the house looks like a cyclone hit it? Family overslept . . . dry cereal bouncing across the kitchen floor . . . Johnny whining about a lost left shoe . . . Susie wiping her runny nose on her sleeve . . . dryer running hot. . . . And Mom. . . .

The devil surely gets to work early some days! He doesn't limit his activities to picking at young mothers, either, though they do seem to be a prime target.

Ask the secretary who has spent the morning searching the files for an elusive paper needed *yesterday,* while everything imaginable comes up in the midst of the search.

Let a schoolteacher unload about the inevitable problem class threatening her composure daily. Talk to the mother of a grumbling, complaining, unappreciative teen-ager. Listen in on the factory supervisor describing absenteeism and what it does to her day. Lend an ear to the club worker burdened with an officer clinging tenaciously to her position but refusing to do a thing about it.

"It's the *little* foxes that spoil the vines," King Solomon said. Wise old man, he knew the nibbling destructiveness of little animals creeping under the hedges of his vineyards. Big animals? No problem!

Big problems? With our fences of courage and determination, let them come! But little upsets? They can be disastrous.

How can we reinforce our "fences" and outwit those little foxes slipping into our lives on every hand, those *little foxes* which threaten and often destroy our serenity?

The most serene women I know are those who have taken preventive measures against upsets. One shared her secret in a retreat last fall. Influenced by a little tract titled "Seven Minutes with God," she practices spending that much time in meditation and prayer before starting her day.

Seven whole minutes! How many women in the midst of the nonstop flight of life in the Space Age have the will power and determination to try it? It's a mere pittance of time, compared to the private devotions of Susanna Wesley, mother of Methodism's John and Charles Wesley. The mother of nineteen children, borne in that many years, Susanna decided after her ninth child came along to set aside two hours a day for communion with God. And commitment made, nothing was allowed to interfere with her appointment.

Some of us would question our ability to set aside a mere seven minutes, much less two hours. But ask any woman who practices regular daily meditation, and she'll tell you the time spent is saved many times over.

A quiet time with God, regularly, can help us develop a customarily good mood, which is, after all, what a good disposition is. Time spent in prayer and seeking him through his Word can sweeten, purify, and transform us. It can engender love—patient, kind, gentle love—in the life, and *love is not easily upset*. The woman who can confront the people and events of her day with love will not be easily provoked, not quickly irritated, not so soon exasperated nor angered.

In this quiet time the Word of God will speak to our need for self-control. It will teach us to live around the things which displease, disturb, and disquiet us. Gradually the wisdom of the Scriptures becomes a way of life for us.

Then, when a husband's hard to live with or a fellow employee is next to impossible, we can test the Bible's teaching that "a soft answer turneth away wrath." When we tend to slacken off and procrastinate, "Let everything be done decently and in order" brings us to our senses. When we're tempted to let our dispositions degenerate into ill humor, we remember, "A merry heart doeth good like a medicine." When we feel like lashing out at those dearest to us, "As ye would that men should do to you, do ye likewise" floats up from somewhere in our subconscious. And the fruit of the Spirit called self-control matures.

A second preventive measure is planning. Some women incorporate this with their meditation, believing plans made under God's guidance are more likely to be effective. However you handle it, planning is good insurance against those upsetting mornings which send whole families on their way late and cross. One young mother declares she starts on Thursday getting her family ready for Sunday—with dress-up clothing clean and pressed, shoes polished, socks sorted. Saturday evening finds her with her alarm set early enough to get the day underway without too much rush. She is the kind with a place-for-everything-and-everything-in-its-place, including Sunday School quarterlies, Bibles, and offering envelopes.

As our daughters were growing up, planning paid off in enlisting their help around the house. Early Saturday morning I would make a "things to do" list, then call the girls to take turns choosing and initialing the tasks for which they'd assume responsibility. They got great satisfaction from crossing off tasks as they were completed. The plan helped prevent the upsets often attendant to children and chores, as well as the upset of coming to the end of the week with a disorganized household.

Today a "things to do" list on the kitchen chalkboard jogs my memory about odds and ends of phone calls, notes, and promises I might otherwise forget. Usually, I find, if a task is important enough to list, it will eventually be accomplished. Or if I look at it long enough, I may decide it's not important after all and in a moment of abandonment scratch it forever from my thinking!

The ability to plan, and to work the plan, is one of the magic ingredients in well-ordered living, whether one is a woman in the business or professional world, a community or church leader, a homemaker—or all three.

When does a full schedule (beneficial, I find, to good mental health) become an overcrowded one? How does one know when her list of things to do is too long?

The demands upon a woman can be overpowering. We are assaulted from every side with a variety of interesting, uplifting, enlightening, and worthy activities. Additionally, a mother is affected by her family's choices, for when mealtimes are interrupted and transportation is required, when clothing must be readied and money doled out, a mother's schedule is bound to be disarranged.

Then, she has her own self to reply to.

All of us have witnessed—and some have experienced personally—the rapid demise of the woman who couldn't say no to leadership responsibility and who was forced to abdicate her position in midterm.

A professional woman who works with women volunteers has come to the conclusion that a woman should hesitate and give careful thought to each new activity under consideration. It takes times, she notes, to weigh each invitation to participate against our present personal involvement and our families' commitments and against our value system. So often, however, we're so busy with previous commitments we don't take time to make wise judgments about future ones.

Is it selfish for a mother or wife to say no in the interest of her serenity? Indeed not, when you consider that "the mother is the heart of the home," and that the quality of a home depends on who and what is at its heart.

Is it selfish for a career woman, recognizing her physical, mental, and emotional limitations, to say no in the interest of a serenity which enables her to cope graciously with daily work situations?

I do not believe Jesus' command to deny self and follow him ignored the varying needs of individuals for time "to be." A woman's life can be rendered ineffective when she overextends herself. Good planning and a watchdog attitude against over-planning are effective preventives against an upsetting way of life that can result in nervousness, ulcers, migraines, and physical and mental breakdowns.

Still another preventive against upsets practiced by many women

is the conscious creating of serene surroundings. Some women seem
to come by the talent naturally, while most of us have to work at the
task.

Some, mostly "morning persons," I suspect, manage to set an atmosphere of serenity by getting up a few minutes ahead of the family
and getting a head start on the day. Others heartily agree with Carol
G. Eisen, who comments in her book, *Nobody Said You Had to Eat
Off the Floor: The Psychiatrist's Wife's Guide to Housekeeping,* "Getting up in the morning is a dreadful job in itself." She suggests the
alternative of doing everything possible the night before. (Incidentally, for women whose upsets seem to hang on their housekeeping
"un-routine," her amusingly written book does contain some sound
advice).

Career women who make a practice of being at their desks a few
minutes early, and of arriving a few minutes ahead of schedule for
appointments, say this gives them a sense of serenity and an upperhand over upsets.

Then, a touch of beauty can help the serenity cause in your life:
a carefully laid table, an attractively served meal, a thriving house
plant, a fresh flower in a sparkling vase. As a business woman, I
noticed the appreciative response of fellow workers to the fresh flowers I brought to my desk from early spring to late fall. For me, they
extended my daily horizon beyond the four walls of the office. And
I'll always cherish the ecstatic reaction of Maria, our Brazilian librarian, when she glimpsed pansies floating among violet leaves in
an oval green glass dish: "Oh-h-h, Martha! That reminds me of a
Brazilian pool!" The effect had taken only minutes to create.

Just as beauty is beneficent, so clutter affects many persons ad-
versely. The clutter in offices, schoolrooms, churches, and yes, homes,
throughout our land, if suddenly scattered to the four winds, would
cause environmental enthusiasts to collapse completely. Dissarray has
a jarring effect on many persons, while order contributes to efficiency
and pleasantness.

We thing-conscious Americans could take a lesson from the Japanese, with their simplicity in home furnishings. We must be ever

watchful lest we clutter up our lives with too many things. For things must be looked after, stepped over, dusted, repaired. Thoreau, who managed to maintain a masterful upperhand over things, once remarked: "I had three pieces of limestone on my desk, but I was terrified to find that they required to be dusted daily, when the furniture of my mind was all undusted still, and I threw them out the window in disgust."

We can so surround ourselves with our treasures that the furnishings of our minds and spirits may be woefully neglected. Jesus Christ said it this way, "Where your treasure is, there will your heart be also." The practice of removing everything from a room once in a while, and then thoughtfully putting back only what we really want is conducive to serenity. Otherwise, we may find empty space in our houses practically nonexistent. And, as a gardening book tells flower-growers, "Empty space is equivalent to silence, a component of elegance."

These days many otherwise elegant homes are sadly wanting for silence. With washer, dryer, blender, kitchen exhaust, garbage disposal, television, and radio going indoors and the neighbor's lawn mower outside, little wonder women are upset by the least additional distraction. The sounds of the city, too, creep in through closed windows and doors. Thankfully government and industry are beginning to study the harmful effects of sound upon man and to search for solutions. But we can exercise some control over inside sounds by planning for quietness.

Even the sounds of good music from the stereo can be improved with intermittent sounds of silence. Women in offices and shops where music is piped into every nook and cranny might ask for fifteen-minute intervals of "nothing" to rest the weary ears of people working there.

God's creatures were built for much more silence than we enjoy today. Its values are extolled in his Word:

". . . he leadeth me beside the still waters."

". . . in quietness and in confidence shall be your strength. . . ."

"Be still and know that I am God . . ."

If we're serious about raising our serenity-level, we must make judgments about the sound level of our surroundings and take steps to build serenity into our homes.

The effective use of lighting and color, too, can help create an environment conducive to serenity. A businessman described his sense of pleasure—and serenity—on coming home to a softly lighted, orderly home after a frantic day at his desk. Psychologists and interior decorators remind us of the effect of color on individuals. Generally, one decorator said, we can get our cue from God's use of color in the universe—those he has used most lavishly are restful, peaceful, serene (and here may I plug my favorite, green!); the hot, bright hues he has used with a dash, as accents. On the other hand, man-made, psychedelic colors have a notably erratic effect, and some studies have pointed to the adverse effects of their use in children's rooms.

While we're on the subject of the senses and serenity, what about the sense of smell? Can you equate the smell of fresh baked bread and chicken stewing on the range with serenity? Sam Levinson suggests a child coming home to the smell of good things cooking in the kitchen might find here the "something missing" that has sent so many youths in search of stimulation through drugs.

Dr. Marion Hilliard, in her excellent book *Women and Fatigue,* says: "It is becoming more and more difficult to make a home—a place of rest, refreshment, nurture, contentment." But it is a challenge deserving our best efforts.

While an ounce of prevention is worth a pound of cure, nevertheless it's a good idea to have some cures handy for the upsets that sneak into our lives like little foxes. Let's take a look at a few multi-purpose cures which have worked to bring serenity to others.

For years my Aunt Harriet, widowed while still a young woman, ran a boarding house, with a few roomers thrown in. The boarders had a habit of dropping in early to sit in her pleasant living room or, in summer, to drape themselves comfortably over porch rockers and swing. The chatter was endless as they waited for their dinner. They liked to stick their noses around the kitchen door, greet her and the kitchen help, inquire about what was cooking and comment accordingly. Her mealtime rush hour did not preclude two young sons presenting her with the usual (and sometimes unusual) problems attendant to little boy living.

"How do you ever manage to keep so calm?" I asked her one day.

"When things get too much for me, I just pretend I'm in a room all alone for a little while," Aunt Harriet replied. "My imaginary room is handy, for I can move it around with me, whenever and wherever I need it."

A physical retreat was out of the question, so she built a retreat in her mind.

Years later, I read of a similar trick for finding peace in the midst of troubling situations, the suggestion being to recall a specially peaceful scene from one's past. I tried it, picking the memory of a late afternoon in the South Mississippi hills when I had gone with another aunt, while on a visit, down to the pasture to bring up the cows. The smell of the pines, unfamiliar to me then, still lingers, and I can still sense the touch of the cool green grass as I stretched out momentarily to look skyward through needled branches. The sound of the tinkling cow bells in the distance and a mental image of the long shadows alternating with lengths of waning sunlight still come back over the years at the thought of that magic moment.

Obviously, such retreats are only second best to actually removing oneself from the scene of an upset, but they are better than none! A department store supervisor tells me she actually removes herself from aggravating situations as rapidly as possible. She goes to her desk and sits down, alone, for awhile.

"The manager upstairs says, 'Let 'em have it!' But I can't. I get a cup of coffee, get off to myself, think the problem over, and pray. I have five girls working for me, and I believe they appreciate me for it. I know I shouldn't be on the floor when I'm upset."

We in our modern homes, without a garden to tend or chickens to feed, do not have the natural retreats of other generations. Nor do we have sisters, aunts, and mothers to relieve us of responsibility from family when things get too much for us. Our children do not have

the retreats their rural counterparts of other times enjoyed—the orchard, the creek, the play spots well away from adult eyes.

Many of today's homes are built with so much openness that it's
difficult to shut oneself away from others, except in an undersized
bedroom built only for sleeping. The vital need for privacy has been
overlooked by many architects, and this has sent many families
scurrying below ground to finish off their basements as areas for
relaxation and refuge.

The upsets created by conflict with other personalities are fed by
the constant proximity of those personalities (yes, Junior included).
It takes two to quarrel, to disagree, to grate on the nerves. And often
we must manage to beat a swift retreat, if only into silence, while those
around us, or we ourselves, simmer down. Which reminds my husband, he says, of the man who never quarreled with his wife; he always
took a walk when trouble was brewing. Drily he adds, "He must have
lived an outdoor life!" The wise author of Proverbs knew the princi-
ple: "Where no wood is, there the fire goeth out. . . ."

Young women today must plan their retreats—whether to the
church, the "Y," the nearest adult education class, the bowling lanes,
or to a part-time job. Today's nuclear family must make some provision for the youngsters so Mother can get away for awhile. And what
a shame to wait until she's "going out of her mind," "tearing her
hair," "climbing the walls," or "ready to scream" before doing something about her need to retreat.

Many men reach for the evening paper or the work in their attache
cases in retreat, and lots of folks switch on television for the same
purpose. One mother insists upon a daily forty-minute snooze for
herself and the children. She suggests a nap but requires quietness.

Every man, woman and child needs a serenity break at least once
daily. It has both preventive and curative qualities. It's a real security
blanket against upsets.

Another simple, but often overlooked, cure for upsets is what my
sister, with a background in the nursing profession, calls "hydrotherapy." When her little ones get cross, she suddenly announces
bathtime, and the warm splashy moments in the tub calm and relax

them into good humor. A more costly but similarly effective remedy is to be found at country club, neighborhood, or backyard pool, with the warmth of the sun providing an added booster to the therapy.

Verifying the value of hydrotherapy in the treatment of upsets, one woman vows that washing dishes, with that sudsy hot water up to her elbows, has a similar effect on her. Lucky woman!

Laughter, too, has a curative effect in upsetting situations. If you can manage to laugh, you may be able to keep from crying. A well-honed sense of humor can redeem you on those days when "everything nailed down seems to be coming loose." Says Arthur Gordon, in "The Engaging Art of Laughing at Yourself": "Certainly the gift of self-mockery is a marvelous catalyst when it comes to easing household tensions. Parents who can laugh at themselves are far more likely to have a warm relationship with their children than parents who cannot. And since such humor is highly contagious, the children learn not only to be amusing themselves; they also acquire an emotional resilience that will be invaluable to them later on."

Erma Bombeck, whose column, "At Wit's End," amuses millions of potentially upset housewives daily, has capitalized on her ability to laugh at herself. Describing life with a two-year-old, "a bald baby a yard high with a smile that could defrost Mt. Everest," she pictures the morning when, among other things, he "ate a guppy, pulled over the flour canister . . . and talked 15 minutes without operator assistance to a housewife in New Mexico." At this particular writing she was following hubby's advice to concentrate on things other than the pain she was enduring. She proudly pointed to her agility at reciting the Declaraction of Independence and the alphabet (backward) and a list of the vice presidents, ending for reasons she did not delineate, with Alben Barkley.

The refusal to overreact to trying situations can be a lifesaver. We sometimes make mountains out of molehills, believing every wild scheme our teen-agers cook up will come to pass. To keep quiet when they test their unlikely-to-be-completed plans on you isn't easy, but time takes care of most of them. The ability to tune out comes in handy for mothers of noisy pre-teeners and talkative three-year-olds (one survey found an average of fifteen thousand words exchanged daily between three-year-olds and their mothers—no record of the number of parental no's reported). We sometimes must make ourselves impervious if we are to survive with serenity. A certain quality of detachment that keeps one aloof from and unruffled by the swirling words surrounding us is desirable.

Maxwell Maltz, in *Psycho-Cybernetics,* maintains that over-response is a bad habit which can be cured. Provoking situations which trigger irritable comebacks or perpetual nagging can be met with *no response.* But a conscious effort must be put forth if we are to break, or unlearn, the habit of reacting negatively. Once over the shock at our failure to react, our antagonist, on not getting a rise out of us, will look for other forms of amusement. We see the effectiveness of refusal to react in the life of Christ, who frequently handled his adversaries by "answering them nothing."

If upsets recur repeatedly in discernible patterns, they will not be cured without accurate diagnosis. One father put his finger on the pulse of the biggest problem in his household, called the phone company and had the service disconnected. At last report, peace reigned between parents and youngsters, and any inconvenience created by a phoneless home was minor in comparison to the problems which arose when their number was in service!

Numerous families, suffering the effects of undisciplined use of television, have delayed repairs and found serenity as they readjusted to a nonspectator kind of existence. When the problem has been diagnosed, decisive action may be indicated, and major surgery may be required.

A final suggestion for the cure of upsets, and one which presents itself repeatedly as we examine the life-situations that lead to unserenity, is what someone has called the "way of acceptance." A friend, relating an experience most women face at one time or another, revealed the beauty of this way of life.

Celista's mother had broken her hip twice, and following her hospitalization had to have constant care. Celista brought her invalid mother into her home, made her room bright and comfortable, and for months gave herself unreservedly to her care. An active woman in church and community affairs, Celista laid all aside without frustration. In contrast to so many who complain about caring for the elderly who no longer can care for themselves, she entered into the experience wholeheartedly.

"Mother said she'd never been powdered so much in all her life! And the neighbors came and went with fresh flowers and delicious food. I'd get things in order and invite church groups in to visit and meet with us. I believe Mother, who'd always before been busy caring for others, actually enjoyed her convalescence. And I enjoyed her stay with us. It was a time for loving and caring for her even as she'd cared for me as a child."

No one needed murmur "poor dear" about Celista. Though the circumstances created by her mother's accident altered the course of her life for a few months, as a maturing Christian she had the ability to calmly accept and to effectively adapt to what could have been very frustrating and irritating to a more selfish and less mature person. What might be termed "upsets" by some women are never recognized as such by others who have learned the way of acceptance.

The upsets which confront us might be compared to the tiny scratches one finds on sterling silver that has been used for years rather than stored. Experts tell us that sterling improves with age and use, for this is how the patina that collectors prize is developed. Even so, the sheen of serenity develops in the life of every woman who learns how to live through and around the inevitable disturbances that arise in the process of her self-giving to others.

3
Dealing with Discontent

"What kind of gift is life unless
we have spirits to enjoy it and
taste its true flavor . . . ?"
—Thoreau

"Honey . . . will you help me move this sofa?"

There she goes again. Never satisfied. The little woman is on a furniture-moving spree, and she knows she's in for some kidding.

The discontents of women—and men—have always preceded progress. The vision of a "better way" has spurred discontented individuals to discoveries and inventions which have eased the brunt of man's battle with his environment. The crusading malcontents of every generation have initiated humane reforms in society which otherwise would never have been accomplished. Someone has pointed out even "the splendid discontent" of God with the formless void from which he created the universe.

Constructive discontent sends a woman on a redecorating binge, makes her "do something" about her hair, goads her into self-improvement through education or weight reduction, pushes her into volunteer service.

Sorrowing discontent with the status quo of her sinful self moves her toward God, to repentance of sin and to faith in the forgiving power of the Savior, to belief in his ability to lead her into paths of successful living.

But "hand-wringing discontent" is the misery which has beset so many American women of our time. Negative discontent has never been more prevalent. Our nation is filled with discontented women, and many of them are members of our Lord's church.

There have always been and always will be women who apparently are born whiners, women who enjoy being miserable. Maybe the blame can be laid to their body build, their metabolic make-up, or the condition of their stomach. Or, growing up under the influence of a discontented mother, they may have arrived at the conclusion early in life that this is the way women are expected to behave.

The mental capacities of today's woman have been expanded far beyond those of her feminine forebears. But a comparable ability to make necessary adjustments to nuclear-age living has not always accompanied such progress. The fault is not altogether her own. The American way of life has been so drastically and rapidly changed by technological advance that many people—of both sexes and of every age—are still struggling to adapt.

Daily, women are made aware that there is so much with which to be discontent. Advertisements describing the perfect house and the happy housewife create dubitable images of happiness. The imperfections in one's own life are accentuated. Articles on child rearing leave today's woman frustrated, uncertain and insecure in her relationships with her children. Soap operas and confessions may contribute to a chronic distrust and dissatisfaction with her mate.

Compound these influences with the unprecedented leisure time housewives today enjoy. Little wonder women become discontent. Add to this the thing-oriented society in which we live, and there's more misery. Subtract the exercise and fresh air grandmother probably received in the course of her workday which must be consciously sought by modern woman. No wonder women grow dull and restless —and discontent.

Dr. John A. Schindler, in his book, *How to Live 365 Days a Year,* says that living in chronic dissatisfaction is about as close to living in hell as anything the world has to offer.

To be ambitious for contentment is, according to the Bible, most worthwhile for the Christian woman. For "godliness *with contentment* is great gain *(should yield dividends).* "A modern translator puts it: "Of course, there's a big profit in religion *if* we're satisfied" . . . and another, "godliness is great gain *provided* it goes with a contented spirit." Note the condition. The fringe benefits of Christian living evidently depend upon us, not upon God. There seems to be some question about Christianity's benefits to the individual *(at least in the here-and-now),* if the believer's faith does not create a sense of inward sufficiency.

Can there be true godliness without contentment?

Is contentment necessary to godliness?

Is godliness necessary to contentment?

Is a restless, discontented woman ever truly a godly woman?

What about the so-called believers who are thoroughly miserable with themselves, their families, their churches, their circumstances?

Discontent suggests resentment, a restless unhappiness. Contentment is a peace which takes care of problems as they arise and does not disintegrate when solutions are not available. Contentment implies an inner attitude that is not disquieted or disturbed by a desire for what one does not possess, even though every wish is not fully gratified.

But can contentment be cultivated, acquired?

If so, how?

A close examination of the minor discontents that clutter the lives of women indicates that many result from a faulty outlook. Consider, for example, a common garden-variety type—discontent with the weather. Every morning when we waken, there is the weather, creeping in through drawn drapes. Every evening when we go out, it is there. And from early 'til late, the public weathermen and their self-appointed allies, our casual acquaintances, keep us posted. People who enjoy wet water at the beach and cold snow on the ski slopes pollute offices and elevators with complaints about the weather.

Few of us have been so fortunate as one little woman in a Missouri home for aging who told the superintendent's wife, "When we children used to peer out the window and complain on dark, gloomy days, Mother always told us to think of 'grey silk—grey silk, so soft and smooth and satisfying to the touch.'" Decades later, this little girl now grown old and feeble continues to see 'grey silk.'

Nor do many of us enjoy the outlook of a waitress in Birmingham, Alabama, who, when I lamented at breakfast about the rainy day, countered kindly, "It's just a mawnin' rain, ma'am," and with her comment transformed the mud into moisture for the tulips and azaleas I admired as I went on my way.

No use complaining!

Out of a construcive discontent, however, man has learned to cope with the weather. With suitable clothing, temperature and humidity controls, snow tires and salt, no problem!

But many women who faithfully check the time and temperature every morning before dressing for the day and who wouldn't think of living in a home without thermostatically controlled heating and cooling, are settling for a life-climate that apparently has no controls. Preferring the luxury of misery, they refuse to be creative in using their inner resources to make a "go" of life.

Self-control, or life-control, can take care of a lot of the discontent that nags at today's woman. Self-control is a kind of inner thermostat with which we can thoughtfully, carefully regulate our attitudes and reactions.

I recall vividly the discovery of how self-control could regulate the quality of my life. Our two daughters were home from college for the summer, and our high-schooler was "around the house." The older girls had been fortunate enough to find summer jobs, and I was continuing to hold down my position at school, with reduced hours, in order to help meet college expenses. My husband's demanding profession had not let up one iota in consideration of the busy season at home.

We lived next door to the church, and between doorbells and knocks at the basement entrance, the telephone, stereo, piano, TV, and radio—well, to say the least, it was all beginning to tell on me!

On a series of mornings I had wakened bad-humoredly, inexcusably cross with the family.

Then, I got a message, and though it wasn't from the Word of God, I believe it was truly divine. On a little rectangle of notebook paper, backed with a bit of orange construction paper, our eldest daughter, Pat, had thumbtacked these hand-printed words to the bulletin board in our breakfast nook: "How beautiful a day can be when kindness touches it."

One miserable Christian woman saw herself that morning and determined to get control of herself. I discovered that inner thermostat—self-control—something that had been available all the time but which I was not using to meet a practical need in my life. All my "goodness"—caring for my family, church work and worship, and clean living—was not producing very much contentment for me or those about me.

We develop and practice self-control in order to achieve in other areas. A cook, baking a pie, doesn't haphazardly throw unmeasured ingredients together, just hoping a mouth-watering dessert will result. A secretary rolling stationery into her typewriter exercises control in turning out a perfect letter. A nurse knows good patient-care doesn't just happen, she controls results by following proven procedures. A teacher plans for a controlled learning situation so she and the class may move toward established goals. A good saleswoman exerts control and care in displaying merchandise and in dealing with customers.

But how often we fail to master, to control, our personal response to circumstances that disturb and disquiet us! We have mastered techniques in many areas, all the while neglecting personal self-control. And I believe it is a special responsibility for women, because the woman in a home generally sets the climate for family living.

The creative use of time is another remedy for discontent. Betty Friedan, in laying the groundwork for woman's liberation, may have overdrawn, and added to, the picture of discontent among American women, but she is unquestionably correct in saying that many housewives do, in varying degrees, suffer from that "trapped" feeling. (Lest one get the notion that only housewives feel "trapped," listen to what one career woman says: "They think we women in the business and professional world have it made, that we are utterly content and happy. They don't know we wear a mask.")

That trapped feeling, however, isn't inevitable. Women have never before had the freedom of choice they enjoy today. But some are still sitting around, or running around, whining and hand-wringing away the best years of their lives.

Women who refuse to use their time creatively have too much time to think—about whether they're doing this or that correctly, whether they're measuring up to some elusive ideal of the model wife and mother, whether they're happy or not.

On the other hand, women who *are* using their time well are usually contented women. Maybe it's true that "happiness is that peculiar sensation you develop when you are too busy to be miserable."

Activity—too much or too little—does affect contentment. In an office building a few years ago I watched the effect of too little activity on a group of employees. Old, water-stained beige drapes covered one wall in our department. Every now and then, we women, and even some of the more sensitive men, would get on a complaining kick about those beige drapes. Why didn't the company do something about them? They were horrible, depressing! We hated them! Then, first thing we knew, the busy season was on us and drapes were forgotten. Just as soon as we got our noses to the grindstone, we forgot them. The same thing happens in homes.

Much of the discontent among women is found in those who have families, yet who, with every imaginable appliance and ready-mix close at hand, do not have enough work to occupy their minds. Their husbands and children leave early for work and school. Hours later, they return, husband with an overflow of work in his attache case, children with homework to do or extracurricular activities to attend. These women often do not have the companionship of sisters, aunts or parents—the extended family—in their home or even in their community, as did women of other days. (Or, if they do, they may still be discontent, not knowing how to use these personal relationships.) In the depersonalized urban areas they may not know their neighbors, and they may go week after week to the supermarket and shopping mall without seeing a single soul they recognize. Tasks like carrying water from the village well or laundering in a common stream which once brought women together in a fellowship are a thing of the faraway past.

A void in the lives of millions of American women has been created

by technological progress. Little wonder those who have not discovered meaningful ways of filling that void grow discontent under the
"just a housewife" routine.

Apart from a return to the good old days, and who wants that, what
are the alternatives?

A career? In *The Christian Woman in the Working World* I explored the possibilities for fulfilment through employment and the
tremendous potential for influence of the Christian woman in the
world beyond the home.

Part-time employment? A study of the effects of technology and
its big baby, urbanization, on drug and alcohol dependents, and juve-
nile delinquents convinces me that the mother who has a choice is
wise not to burden herself with full-time employment. It is difficult
to give quality care to children and young people in a home when
the feet hurt and the energy level is low. When one is emotionally
drained from a day among many people, too little of the self is left
for mothering. The hours until it's time to get up and go again are
all too short for the tasks left waiting at home.

About ten years ago a national organization called Catalyst was
formed to encourage young women to plan ahead for the successive
phases of their lives and to alert educated women and potential employers to the possibilities of women combining rewarding work with
family responsibility. Experiments and research have been conducted
revealing tremendous possibilities in part-time work for women with
children under eighteen in the fields of education, social work, industry and science—to the advantage of women and society as well.

What about volunteer service? For the woman with time on her
hands, here is an outlet for energies being dissipated by discontent.
No longer is volunteer service the prerogative of the wealthy, upper-
middle class American woman. Today women from every strata of
society are playing "Lady Bountiful."

The woman who prefers to give herself first and foremost to her
family, but who finds she's climbing the walls in desperation when
she limits her attention to family and home may discover a great sense
of serenity and contentment as she discovers her niche in a challeng-

ing volunteer effort. Some women find their niche in Sunday School classes or youth organizations. Mission action groups in many churches furnish a wide selection of opportunities for church-related volunteer service. Community agencies of every sort are crying out for volunteers. Today one out of every four Americans serves as a volunteer in some five hundred thousand individual agencies throughout the nation. They assist with family and child welfare, recreation, education, health, housing and urban renewal, in hospitals and the field of correction, as well as in church-related positions. This tremendous army of people of good will are helping achieve important societal goals as they work with professionals to improve the nation's economy, politics, education, and social welfare.

The woman with a big family, on a shoestring budget, sewing, cooking, housekeeping, may not dare look beyond her yard for additional activity. But she can find her contentment in seeing the ripple of influence for a better world beginning in her home. Ashley Montagu in his book, *The Natural Superiority of Women,* points out the dignity of such responsibility: "Women are the mothers of humanity . . . do not let us ever forget that, or underemphasize its importance. What mothers are to their children, so man will be to man."

A beginning place for contentment is that moment when a woman moves out and away from selfish concerns and self-interest to do something for another. Unselfishness is becoming and highly gratifying to mother, wife, relative, friend, employee, or to the woman seeking out a helping relationship to someone yet unknown to her.

A. H. Maslow, in a study of healthy, highly fulfilled, mature individuals, whom he terms "self-actualizing," notes: "These individuals customarily have some mission in life, some task to fulfil, some problem outside themselves which enlists much of their energies." He points out that self-actualizing persons, involved in useful, meaningful activity, somehow never stale in their enjoyment of day-to-day living and are untouched by the trivialities which create so much discontent in others.

When that "mission in life, that task to fulfil, that problem outside

ourselves" begins to wear on us, it's wonderful to turn away to something for fun. One of the most valuable lessons I've learned from my
mother is the worthiness of a hobby. Her life has not been easy this
last quarter of a century. She assumed the care of two elder sisters
and this responsibility stretched into many years. Hardening of the
arteries and senility are not easy to live with. But Mother had her
garden. It was escape. It was freedom. It was contentment. For years
her church was adorned with her beautiful, often elaborate arrangements. A horticulture expert, her phone has been busy with friends
and acquaintances calling for information and advice. Last Christmas
she polished some of the silver trays and bowls she has received as
awards in flower shows and gave them to her children. Mother's
fingers are stiff now; she says she can no longer do much with arrangements. Her knees ache and she can't get down and clean out her
hemerocallis beds as she used to do. But she's invested in a fluores-
cent-lighted cart and now specializes in African violets.

In imitation of my mother, I've converted the bare yard of our
parsonage home into a colorful summer scene. As springtime comes
to the Rockies I'll be out digging, the sun warm on my back, between
paragraphs of this book. In the room where I write geraniums bloom,
from my first attempt with cuttings. And in the kitchen window over
my sink, snapdragons are sprouting from seed, another new experience for me. Like Mabel Barbee Lee, ". . . I confess to a love of
gardening and what it has done in giving me a sense of belonging,
of freedom and tranquillity that are so vital to all human beings. The
land has been mine, no matter who owned it. . . ."

Too often we women are so perfection-oriented that we hesitate to
take up a hobby. But we don't have to be top-notch to have fun.
Whether it's ceramics, dressing dolls, or breadmaking, the value of
a hobby is in the enjoyment, the contentment, one derives from it.
If we aren't careful, the drive for excellence can spoil all the fun.
Hobbies are primarily for *doing,* not for *showing,* for the performer,
not her audience.

Keeping busy, however, is no guarantee against discontent, even
when work is purposeful and you've a hobby waiting for your leisure

time. Monotonous routine can produce a discontented woman. It can happen at home. The sameness of daily chores—wash, iron, clean, cook—day in, day out! It can happen in a job, and even the most exciting has its chore-like aspects. Monotony can send a woman to a doctor and unless her physician knows how she is spending her days he may overlook the one factor which is creating her enormous fatigue.

If a monotonous routine is about to get you down, look around and see what you can change. If you're a homemaker, move the furniture, change the seating arrangement at the dinner table, go to the dime store and buy some new place mats! If you're a typist and you rearranged your desk yesterday, try taking a different route to work tomorrow. Sit near a different girl on coffee break. Or change your margin stops!

Whatever you do, don't allow boredom to linger. LaVerne Hull, better known to Iowans as "Mrs. Trotting Shoes," says, "When I meet women who seem to be bored with life, I itch and long to advise them to (a) get a new hairdo; (b) buy something bright red, if only a new scarf; (c) try a new recipe; (d) get enough sleep, an adequate diet, and a good walk every day; (e) read a good book; (f) go to church as if it were a new experience. All, part, or a combination of these probably would cure all but the really hopeless."

Suppose we have developed a remarkable degree of self-control in daily circumstances. Let's assume we're not sitting around idly day after day. Still discontent?

Could it be that "wanting" impulse?

Remembering Eve, we realize we *are* wanting creatures. Without this urge, we might not survive. The problem is, where do we draw the line?

Like other normal drives, wanting can easily get out of hand. Desire can become obsession.

Aware of our problem, God delivered a warning against excessive "wanting." The tenth commandment, given to women today might read, "You shall not covet your neighbor's house, your neighbor's husband, her labor-saving appliances, her automobile, or anything that is your neighbor's."

Jesus underscored the original command and advised further: "Guard yourselves and keep free from all covetousness—the immoderate desire for wealth, the greedy longing to have more; for a woman's life does not consist and is not derived from possessing overflowing abundance, or that which is over and above her needs."

Paul gives further emphasis, "Kill (deaden, deprive of power) the evil desire lurking in your members"—and he includes greed and covetousness in his list of impulses that make for sin. He calls covetousness a form of idolatry—"the deifying of self and other created things instead of God."

Bringing the problem up-to-the-minute, Martha Patton, a syndicated columnist, describes a family whose life had become a picture of the wife's greed. "Their houses, cabinets, and closets fairly bulged with her purchases. . . . Everywhere you looked, another acquisition sprouted. When she ran out of places to put things, she didn't stop adding things—she added places."

The Christian woman with her eyes set on the "eternals" will refuse to be manipulated by the passing fancies of the fashion world, the furniture business, and every other imaginable organization dedicated to a sales-minded god. She will not be bogged down by debt and discontent.

She develops the attitude of gratitude. She knows God is the giver of every good and perfect gift. She sees her very breath and life as a gift from the Creator. She is grateful for her relationship with the Father made possible by her faith in his Son. She finds in the simple things of life much to be enjoyed, and she is appreciative. She stops frequently to count her blessings.

The popular painting "Grace," hanging in dining areas in countless homes depicts the attitude of gratitude better than the proverbial ten thousand words. An old man bows in thanksgiving to God. His meal? Only a bowl of porridge.

In contrast to the discontents arising from dissatisfaction with externals, some women experience an unhealthy, hand-wringing dis-content with themselves. A healthy self-esteem is absolutely essential to serenity. We have to learn, if it does not come naturally, to love and respect ourselves, to actually like ourselves. Only as we arrive at an evaluation of ourselves and reach firm decisions about the direction we wish our lives to take and *begin to move* in that direction, will we begin to like ourselves.

An old woman, haunted by the vague idea of a mysterious content-ment with which other people were gifted but which was denied her, made life completely miserable for herself and everyone around her.

After many years of turbulent living, one day she did an about-face. She began to smile, to be pleasant. When someone finally got up the courage to ask what had brought about such a drastic change in her personality, she replied, "I don't know. All my life I've been a-strain-ing and a-struggling to have a contented mind like other folks. Finally, I decided to settle down and be contented without one."

If you are troubled by a negative discontent which is destroying your serenity, the suggestions offered in this chapter might be summed up as a seven-sided approach to the problem—

- A positive mental attitude
- An acceptance of what cannot be changed
- A determined life control
- The creative use of time
- A sound philosophy about material possessions
- An attitude of gratitude
- A healthy regard for oneself

4

Overcoming Discouragement

"But O my soul, don't be discouraged!
Don't be upset! Expect God to act!
For I know that I shall again have plenty of
reason to praise Him for all that He
will do! He is my help! He is my God!"
—Psalm 42:11, *The Living Bible, Paraphrased*

"I'm so discouraged I could. . . ."

Cry? Quit? Die?

If you've said it, join the club!

You know discouragement when you see it.

At work your boss sits gazing into space, unable to get down to the business at hand.

Your son comes in from school, discouraged. "What's the use?" he mutters angrily.

Your husband arrives in the evening, shoulders sagging, eyes dull, smile not so quick as usual, irritability ready to surface at the slightest provocation.

Your neighbor calls. "I ripped that zipper out half a dozen times and still don't have it right. And Jack comes in and wants to know why I'm crying. 'Don't get so upset, honey,' he says, 'it's just a hobby. . . .' *His* hobby is model ships and planes—he just doesn't understand!"

A woman from the church confides, "Nobody wants to do anything. Everyone's so busy . . . sometimes I feel like giving up."

Discouragement is hard to disguise. It slips out when we don't plan for it to, spilling over into our phone conversations, coming to light when we meet a friend at the supermarket. It whines its way into our small talk at church, even on festive occasions—wherever we can find a listening ear. It sneers at us through incompleted projects laid aside in desk drawers, closets, and basements.

Discouragement—what is it?

Once upon a time, the devil put some of his tools up for sale. The curious came by droves, and seeing one small, worn tool marked with a huge price, they asked, "What's this little tool you've priced so high?"

"You folks call it discouragement," the devil replied smugly. "The handiest little gadget I've ever owned. I can get into lives with it where nothing else will work. Funny, most folks never guess it belongs to me."

Apparently it's still in his possession. For discouragement continues to slow down the human race, to turn us around, to put us out of commission mentally, physically, and emotionally. We drop out—club and church leaders giving up responsibility, mothers pleading 'What's a mother to do?' employees dragging back and forth half-heartedly to work—living pictures of discouragement.

At times it pushes us downward into dejection, despondency, depression, desperation, despair. . . .

Discouragement seems to come most often to people who expect too much.

We may expect too much of ourselves—perfectionists, compulsive housekeepers, detail-conscious hostesses who can't enjoy our own parties. It's discouraging never to have everything "just so."

We may expect too much of others. We become discouraged with other women whose interests, energies, and capabilities don't measure up to ours, with our youngsters whose values are not so stable nor lofty as ours, with our husband whose ways do not quite suit us.

We may expect too much of life. Our home, our social status, our accumulation of wealth are not quite adding up to the charmed existence of our youthful fantasies.

"It's discouraging," we say.

But while we may be guilty of too high expectations of ourselves, of others, and of life, frequently we are guilty of too low expectations of our God. Struggling with the powers of evil which seek to destroy us through discouragement, we forget we need not do battle alone.

An acquaintance—of what religious faith, if any, I do not know—
hooted when I suggested Christian women should be able to cope.

"Why?" she laughed scornfully. "Because they have something to
lean on?"

I was too shocked to reply. I must have assumed that everyone
knew we have an inner resource upon which we can "lean" (if you
want to call it that), an inner strength which can bring us victoriously
through difficulty and discouraging circumstances.

Maybe she had known some Christian, somewhere, who was not
utilizing that resource. Indeed, maybe some of us have not yet learned
to "lean."

We parrot the phrase, "Christ is the answer." We say we believe
life's answers are in the Bible, that it is the greatest how-to book of
all. We don't always rely on the answers but we know where they
are!

Granted, sometimes the circumstances of life are enough to cause
discouragement. Even women alone, while they may not be limited
by family ties, find themselves hemmed in by circumstances—financial obligations, career boundaries, educational limitations, and
health.

Usually, where a married woman will live, and how, and the way
she will spend the bulk of her time and energy during the mothering
years are dictated by the circumstances of her husband's career. The
circumstances of a woman's life are frequently beyond her control.

But the question is, under the circumstances, how will she live?

Every life has its crises.

Emergencies arise.

And daily, daily, daily the little upsets pick at us like so many little
imps. Christian women are not exempt! And often, far too often, we
are overcome with discouragement. When we are disheartened, our
energies are dissipated, our personalities disintegrate, and around us
people are distressed. If only discouragement weren't contagious!

Modern woman's search for the answers to triumphant, courageous
living may take her to her physician, to a psychiatrist, to her minister,
to the library and bookstore, to conferences on fascinating woman-

hood, or to conclaves of the woman's liberationists. It may send her fleeing to the mountains, the lakes, or the seashore. It may thrust her into the business and professional world, far from the quiet (or turmoil) of her home. It may press her to the point where she reaches more and more frequently into her medicine cabinet for something to pep her up, or calm her down.

The search may drive her to the liquor cabinet, or the drug peddler. It may leave her glassy-eyed before her television set in escape from the realities of life. Or it may force her into hiding, in withdrawal from people, beneath the covers of her bed.

If she is wise, it will lead her into a close scrutiny of her inner self, and fortunate indeed is the woman who resorts to a personal spiritual checkup in her search for serenity.

For as discouragement is the devil's tool, so courage begins with God.

The courage the world offers is like a child's soap bubble. We-can't-quite-get-hold-of-it. Just as we think it's ours, it vanishes.

But the courage which God gives is different. When we put our trust in Jesus Christ, Son of God, a courage of the spirit is born within us, a hope not to be held gingerly lest it disappear, but to carry confidently into every circumstance.

It is a steadfastness born of peace with God, a reserve of strength upon which we can draw when the devil is using our circumstances to try to get us down.

If we can get God's perspective of trials and troubles, we can triumph rather than be beaten down by discouragement. He sees life's hard spots as producing endurance and patience in his children, and he will reinforce our positive reaction to trying circumstances. We can be assured of his commendation when we don't allow discouragement to get the best of us. Knowing of his understanding and his approval, we can move right on into the business at hand, regardless of hardships.

We may as well be realistic about life. If we are taken in by the philosophy of the old round, "Row row row your boat, Gently down the stream, Merrily, merrily, merrily, merrily, Life is but a dream," we're in for a rude awakening. Life is definitely not a downstream voyage, and at times it can be more a nightmare than a dream.

But if we can keep moving, the battle with discouragement is half-licked.

Think of the disagreeable task you keep putting off. Every day it stares up at you from your workbasket at the office or from the sewing table at home, or it nags at you from somewhere within. The longer you look at it, or think about it, the worse it seems. Then, finally, one day you get so disgusted you tackle it with vigor. Pretty soon you are almost (if not quite) enjoying the task. Discouragement begins to disappear.

Heloise, the frustrated housewife's idol and confidante, advises homemakers: "Never sit and worry about what you have to do. If it bothers you that much, get up out of that chair and get it done. The dividends in 'peace-of-mind' are worth the effort." Up-and-at-'em is a good slogan for the business or professional woman, church or club worker, and the would-be volunteer as well. Discouragement can be dispelled with self-discipline.

Work has a way of helping a woman solve many problems. Every task, no matter how small, can bring satisfaction and encouragement when performed with excellence. The expending of physical and mental energy can clear the mind dulled by laziness and inertia. It can lift the spirits made dreary by inactivity and complaining.

An idle mind the devil's workshop? Don't laugh. Remember his favorite tool, discouragement.

When there's a job to be done, you've heard the whisper: "It's no use. You can't. It's too difficult. Quit! Quit! Quit! Or at least, put it off. . . ."

But something within urges, "Keep moving!" The battle is on, and one side is going to win.

Determination is so vital to the victory. It is the power which keeps us functioning under stress, which helps us to sweat out a project or a situation in spite of setbacks or opposition.

*   *   *

Clearly defined goals help to fortify us against discouragement and failure.

A writer in a public relations office, on receiving a new assignment, invariably asked, "Now what's the purpose of the exercise?" Not a bad question for a lot of situations! What's the purpose of a clean, attractive home? of this missions organization I'm leading? of PTA? of den-mothering? of this drive for funds? of this Sunday School class? of this job that claims thirty-odd hours of my precious time every week?

"People have a tendency to lose sight of their goals," says a sales manager of a big organization utilizing woman-power. "I find my women must be reminded periodically why they went to work in the first place. They get their noses so close to their work that they get nearsighted. So now and then I help them get out their purposes where they can see them again, and then together we shine them up and they go away with the urge to try a little harder." This usually gets at the roots of their discouragement.

The "big picture" of our duties can give meaning even to unpleasant, frustrating tasks. The picture of the finished product that comes in our crewel kits keeps us stitching away, even with the colors we don't particularly like, until we've completed the piece. With the full picture in mind we can more easily accept and heartily accomplish the tedious details that are part and parcel of every worthwhile endeavor.

While we may be completely sold on the product toward which we direct our energies, the processes are not always easy and pleasant. As one writer expressed it: "I don't enjoy writing; I enjoy having written." Similarly, we may often have to admit, "I don't enjoy this duty, but I will enjoy whatever it is I am working toward."

A sense of certainty that one's life is being directed by God is one of the finest antidotes for discouragement.

How well I remember that bright October morning several years ago when this truth took on fresh meaning for me. At the time I was disheartened, discouraged with "the way things were going" in my

life. That morning I debated about whether to attend a citywide
missions rally being held in a church across town. It was too late to
invite someone to go along with me, and I didn't want to go alone.
But something propelled me from my dreary routine that day. I didn't
know until she was introduced that an old friend was to speak. She
was home from her post in the interior of Brazil.

"I don't *enjoy* having weevils in the beans," she said, "and having
to board up our windows against thieves. I don't enjoy being alone
with the children and servants when my husband is away. I didn't
enjoy being unable to visit my mother before she died recently. I
haven't enjoyed seeing my son crippled for life for lack of adequate
medical care. Nor being away from family and friends for years at
a time." As she spoke I remembered the discouragement she and her
husband had faced as they sought to meet stringent requirements for
appointment as foreign missionaries, their initial rejection, the years
of continuing preparation before their appointment became a reality.
How ashamed I was as I heard her conclude, "I don't enjoy these
things, but I wouldn't be anywhere else in the world when I know
beyond a shadow of a doubt this is the will of God for us."

All of us do not have the missionary's strong sense of God's will
for our lives. But as Christians we must realize that our purpose in
life should not be self-gratification.

Then, a sense of timing can prevent us becoming easily discouraged.
A patience develops as we realize, with Solomon:

For everything its season, and for every activity under heaven its time:
      a time to be born and a time to die;
      a time to plant and a time to uproot;
      a time to kill and a time to heal;
      a time to pull downward and a time to build up;
      a time to weep and a time to laugh;
      a time for mourning and a time for dancing;
      a time to scatter stones and a time to gather them;
      a time to embrace and a time to refrain from embracing;
      a time to seek and a time to lose;
      a time to keep and a time to throw away;
      a time to tear and a time to mend;

a time for silence and a time for speech;
a time to love and a time to hate;
a time for war and a time for peace.   (Eccl. 3:1–8, NEB)

But we live in what has been called an instant society, in a ready-mix, ready-made environment. While technology has provided us with speedy solutions to the age-old, tedious tasks of cleaning and cooking and washing and ironing, it has deprived us of the experiences that in the past taught women patience. Today the mind is a lot freer to entertain discouragement. The body does not know the kind of physical weariness which washes away self-centeredness and self-pity.

But there are women in our day who live triumphantly. Looking at three in highly diverse circumstances, I notice they have several qualities in common.

They take life as it comes—a day at a time.

One, a professional woman, has her fingers in more pies than dozens of other women combined. She is president of a national organization for women, program chairman of an international alliance of Christians, director of a student center for a huge university, to mention a few of her responsibilities. I asked her how she does it and she replied simply, "I just do what needs to be done one day at a time. I don't let things upset me."

Another carries a different load. With a large family and the constant influx of house guests teen-agers bring, she takes it all in her stride, with little evidence of frustration. How do you do it, her friends marvel. "Just take it as it comes, a day at a time!" she says.

Still another, a business woman handling an unbelievable work load at her office and a heavy emotional load at home with a problem husband and children who are practically her total responsibility, lives with zest and courage. She, too, is a one-at-a-timer.

They have learned to know and accept themselves.

They are aware of their potential and of limitations imposed upon them by health, mentality, endurance, and the circumstances that surround them. From somewhere deep within they have been able to determine what they can and cannot do, what they should and should not attempt. Seeking God's help they may have prayed, "Examine me, O God, and know my thoughts; test me, and understand my misgivings, watch lest I follow any path that grieves thee; guide me in the ancient ways" (NEB).

They realize the search for self-knowledge is a continuing process. For what a woman might be able to accomplish and what might be her heart's desire at one point in her life may be altogether different at another. There is no conflict—it is merely the unfolding of the soul, as Gibran says, "like a lotus of countless petals."

They don't measure themselves by their neighbors or associates. They don't have time to be constantly pulling up their roots to see if they are "growing." They are not trying to impress anyone. Their self-confidence does not depend on what others think of them. They all, however, are concerned that they earn God's approval.

They have learned to be patient with others as they are. They may not *like* (nor approve) all they see, but they do not let what they dislike throw them into discouragement. They are too busy trying to relate effectively to those closest to them.

They have examined the life of Christ and discovered his serene patience—with Judas, the woman at the well, Peter, his brothers —and are seeking to express that same spirit through their own attitudes.

They are women who accept the "inalterables."

They have prayed for wisdom to know the difference between what they can change and what they cannot change. With courage they attack the one and with serenity accept the other. Maybe they have assimilated Reinhold Niebuhr's prayer which has been the life-changing ingredient for thousands upon thousands of discouraged individuals:

> God, grant me
> the serenity to accept the things I cannot change,
> the courage to change the things I can change, and
> the wisdom to know the difference.

These women look upon illness and the other emergencies of life as divine interruptions. They find ways to live through each crisis serenely, making the best of the situation.

They have made mistakes like the rest of us. The professional woman comments: "I should have done it this way. Next time. . . ." The housewife reasons: "If I had only started sooner. . . ." The business woman cries: "Glory hallelujah, I got experience!" And God approves.

They can laugh at themselves and somehow see some flicker of humor in otherwise depressing situations. They are proof that "a merry heart doeth good like a medicine."

They are women who usually manage to get the amount of rest they personally require for maximum performance.

They stand tall in the knowledge that they are God's creation, his handiwork, that he loves them, he even likes them. They can stay on top of their circumstances with this kind of security.

God stands ready to help the Christian woman when discouragement threatens her serenity.

Recently I watched the Word of God at work on discouragement in a woman's life. Sally's husband is not a Christian, and for many years her heart's desire has been to see him become a believer. In a small group who had gathered to pray, we looked together at the story Jesus told about the importunate widow who kept pleading with the unjust judge until he granted her request for aid. We talked of Jesus' teaching that women ought always to pray and not to lose heart. I felt discouragement disappear as Sally prayed, "Lord, help me to be like that little widow woman and not give up about my husband."

Countless disheartened women, advised to read a psalm each morning over an extended period of time, have found in them answers to their discouragement.

The Bible repeatedly encourages the believer, with its accounts of men and women who have taken heart through their personal relationship with God.

But sadly, too many Christian women prefer to enjoy their misery and refuse to resort to the Master's Word for help.

Discouragement comes to every Christian woman, but it need not defeat her. Through willing obedience to God's commonsense commands and an abiding trust in his promises, she can conquer it.

She can experience the same elation Isaiah expressed when, thousands of years ago, he wrote,

> Hast thou not known? hast thou not heard,
> that the everlasting God, the Lord, the Creator
> of the ends of the earth, fainteth not,
> neither is weary?
> there is no searching of his understanding.
> He giveth power to the faint; and to them
> that have no might he increaseth strength.
> Even the youths shall faint and be weary,
> and the young men shall utterly fall;
> But they that wait upon the Lord shall
> renew their strength; they shall mount up
> with wings as eagles; they shall run,
> and not be weary; and they shall walk,
> and not faint.   (Isa. 40:28–31)

She can lean (if you want to call it that) upon his promise:

> Fear thou not; for I am with thee:
> be not dismayed; for I am thy God:
> I will strengthen thee;
> yea, I will help thee;
> yea, I will uphold thee
> with the right hand of my righteousness.   (Isa. 41:10)

5

Coping with Disappointment

"God can do wonders with a broken heart
if you give him all the pieces."
—Victor I. Alfsen

C-R-A-S-H!!! Haven't you stood with your heart in your throat at the sound of something breaking? A lamp, a vase, a pitcher, a plate—something you'd treasured purely for sentimental reasons, or a valuable antique cherished by generations of women in your family. Maybe a bit of glassware you'd fallen in love with at first sight, that had become a part of you from the moment you held it in your hand. And now this part of you—broken!

Crying out in hurt and disappointment, you've stooped to gather up the pieces. With a little glue, can it be salvaged? Or is it shattered beyond repair? Is there hope, or none at all?

The fragile stuff life's made of carries no guarantee against breakage. Nor can one be assured of repairs. Plans, hopes, dreams are dashed. Disappointment. . . .

How does a woman, her heart broken by disappointment, find serenity? My search has taken me to a number of women who, in spite of deep disappointments, have managed to live triumphantly beautiful lives.

In all of them I found an attitude of acceptance. Unlike discouragement which is an emotion or an attitude which can be worked through, disappointment wears an air of finality. Like a broken vase, there it is. It has happened, and there are times when acceptance is the only way to serenity. There's no turning back. Damage from disease, birth-related defects, and accidents cannot always be repaired. The effects of wrong choices cannot always be erased. Death snatches away a loved one. Disappointment. . . .

Acceptance must come. A minister and educator, preaching on the love of God, described intimately the disappointment God must experience when his children do not return his love. He compared it to that of a parent whose severely retarded child can never put his arms around his parents and say, "I love you."

His wife, speaking to a group of young women, assured them of God's abundant grace, bestowed as it is needed. Her words carried a note of authority. She did not have to say, "I know what I'm talking about." They knew that this couple had such a child. But in neither did I detect the slightest note of bitterness, the least tinge of self-pity. They were beautiful people, for they had accepted and risen to meet the challenge of their child's retardation.

A woman whose husband was an alcoholic never questioned whether or not she should continue to live with him. For years, though, she chafed at her disappointment and made excuses for her misery. In shame and self-pity she withdrew from all who could have made life worthwhile. Then one day, with a sudden insight into what her reaction was doing to her children, she did an about-face. "I just decided I might as well accept my husband's problem and make the best of life in spite of it." That decision transformed her home and may have saved her children's future, for their personalities blossomed with her change of attitude.

Still another young woman, rejected by her husband, lived for years knowing of her husband's affairs with other women. Her life was continually torn by doubt, fear, quarreling, and ultimately, financial disaster. Finally she left him to move near the shelter of her parents' love. Faced with the decision about dissolving the marriage contract, she was haunted by the words, "Let no man put asunder." The fact that her husband—and the other women in his life—had long since divided what God had joined did not assuage the disappointment and heartbreak of the broken relationship. The prospects of a one-parent home, of supporting herself and her child, of living alone were frightening. Gradually, however, she found serenity in acceptance. She managed to say through her tears, "Let it be." She took a hard look at the alternatives—bitterness or resignation—and she chose the better of the two. Then she rolled up her sleeves in determination to make the best of the situation.

In a different kind of heartbreak I saw serenity, too. From St. Paul, Minnesota, comes the account of a woman who is watching two of her children, afflicted by a rare disease, slowly becoming human vegetables. This mother said she felt like "everything had been wiped out" when the doctor explained that the disease was gradually destroying the nervous system of the children and that death would probably occur within five years.

Nevertheless, she forced herself to accept the tragedy. "I'm not spending my life asking why, because I never could find that answer," she said. "I'm not going to sit in a chair and become bitter and old. . . . I take every minute and every day one at a time. I do what I have to do because it is a part of my life." She takes care of the children herself, with the constant help of her mother. She jogs, bicycles, and plays volleyball for diversion—the activity helps counteract depression, she says.

Though these stories from real life have tragic overtones, we needn't waste our pity on these women. Each of them has found serenity in circumstances where all hope for wholeness is gone. Each took the giant step of acceptance.

Mary Ann Hamilton, paralyzed from her waist up by polio just before the Salk vaccine was perfected, suggests that when one must abandon hope of a complete reversal of disappointing circumstances, other dreams must fill the void. One must dream a "possible" dream.

"For a long time," she wrote, "complete recovery was the only mountain I dreamed of climbing. But if not all dreams are possible, another can take its place."

Her second-best dream was to be able to go up into the high country which she glimpsed each day as she looked toward the west. "Unless one has grown up in the shadow of the Rockies, he cannot know the magnetic pull drawing his very soul to their cool seclusion. To me, the thought of being cut off from this peace forever was almost unbearable."

But her breath capacity was scarcely sufficient to sustain life at lower elevations, and for years trips into the rarefied atmosphere of the mountains were out of the question. Then, a simple little piece of equipment which expanded her lungs liberated her from the flat-lands. Each summer now, with her head support brace and the loop of cloth which carries her hands, she climbs into the station wagon with husband, four children, and quantities of camping paraphernalia to head west toward Loveland Pass.

"I wonder if I'm out of my mind each time we start up that tortuous route," she says. "I know my chest will feel like petrified wood as the car snakes higher and higher. The scenery is breathtaking, and so is the altitude." Though sometimes they must hurry down, her second-best dream has been realized.

The finest of persons sometimes experience the disappointment of closed doors to a career, and substitution must be made. Career doors don't always swing open as hoped, and splendid men and women prepared by education and experience for specialized work must look for a second-choice of occupation. One couple, after seventeen years as missionaries in the Orient, had to abandon their dreams of a lifetime of overseas service because of the wife's health. Nevertheless, they have found peace and joy in other areas of work. They write: "God is the architect of our lives and we can neither demand to see the blueprint nor ask him to sign on the dotted line that no details of the plan will be changed. . . . God does not make mistakes. . . . God does not waste human personality. . . . He will take any hour or any day we give him and make it into something wonderful and useful."

A second-best dream may have a world of joy and satisfaction in store. Ask the childless woman who has adopted or become a foster-parent. In contrast to the women for whom Mother's Day serves merely as a bitter reminder of their childlessness, so many are finding fulfilment for their mothering instincts through a substitute relation-ship. Today's childless woman, wanting a child, need not carry her disappointment alone, as did Hannah, weeping, grieving, fretting, refusing to eat because she had no child. Adoption regulations are not so stringent as they once were, and agencies have developed uncanny methods of matching children to parents. If hope for bearing a child must be abandoned, by all means investigate the alternatives.

Along with the giant step of acceptance and the frequent use of substitution, I found a big measure of determination in the lives of women who have triumphed over disappointment. The serene ones who impressed me most were not passive creatures. Far from it!

Eleanor Roosevelt is an excellent example. Her childhood was a series of traumatic experiences and disappointing circumstances. Born to physically handsome parents, her mother one of the most popular women in New York society, Eleanor was not a pretty child, a fact that seemed to estrange her from her mother, who sometimes called her "Granny."

She adored her dashing, adventurous father, however, but he was a confirmed alcoholic, and their relationship was disturbed when he was banished by his family to Europe in search of a cure.

While still very young, she was battered by the shock of three deaths: her mother's, a brother's, and her beloved father's in a riding accident.

Eleanor grew up under the care of her maternal grandmother, who forced her to abide by strict rules which set her apart from others her age. No sweets, a steel brace to improve posture, cold baths each morning to prevent colds, hemlines above her knees when others her size wore their dresses at midcalf. A tall, thin, shy girl, she was watched over closely by maids and governesses. Visits with her father's family were prohibited, and she was denied the opportunity to travel with the family of a young friend. Her debut into New York society was so painful it almost caused a nervous collapse.

Nor did marriage to Franklin Delano Roosevelt bring sudden happiness. It was more like "upperclass captivity," for her mother-in-law took over the training and management of her son's wife with such vigor that Eleanor was left feeling helpless. When she remonstrated, her husband said, "Don't be silly." Only when Franklin Roosevelt was stricken with polio did she really assume her rightful role as the woman of her house. Only then, as she threw herself into the rehabilitation of her husband, did she begin to come into her own as a person.

Yet, Joan Erikson writes in her *Notes on the Life of Eleanor Roosevelt,* that in spite of such a childhood and young womanhood, "the woman emerged who more than any other woman in American history played a leading role in public affairs, who gave to the position of the President's wife an entirely new force, the woman who was to become chairman of the committee which drew up the United Nations Declaration of Human Rights. . . ."

Through determination, an act of will, through the setting aside of thought of self and putting her mind intently upon the needs of others around the world, Mrs. Roosevelt seems to have transcended her highly disappointing childhood. One of her favorite quotations may reveal the secret of her poise and composure in the midst of her often-derided efforts: "Back of tranquillity lies always conquered unhappiness."

Note the effort implied. To "conquer" carries the idea of gaining or securing control of, as if by military force; to overcome or surmount by physical, mental, or moral force; to be victorious; to win. It does not imply a lackadaisical walking about, glancing around in search of a pot of happiness at the foot of an ephemeral rainbow.

Multitudes of men and women have accepted their unlikely beginnings and have by sheer determination become conquerors of inalterable circumstance. It's amazing what people have accomplished, when they refused to place a period after their disappointments. Chester Swor, the popular writer and youth counselor whose own example of victory over a severe physical handicap has inspired millions, has gathered into a book entitled *Neither Down nor Out* the thrilling stories of numerous individuals who have proved by their great achievements that no handicap is beyond the power of God and the courage of the individual to conquer. Proof that "the impossible may just take a little longer."

The quality of determination can bring a measure of success to less dramatic, but nevertheless disturbing, circumstances which may culminate in disappointment. For instance, many women have faced up to the fact that their marriage wasn't all it should be and have determined to do what they could to improve it.

They've asked themselves: Have I depended too much on my hus-band, refusing to become a whole person apart from him? Have I demanded he meet me on my terms, or have I stepped across the halfway line to meet him on his? Am I sensitive to and understanding of his needs? Am I available when he wants to talk? Do I dump problems into his lap, or do I do some preliminary thinking in order to reach intelligent decisions? What about my sense of humor? Do I respect his confidence? Have I learned to listen with my heart? Do I show appreciation for him? How often do *I* say, "I love you"?

Not only husband-wife relationships, but those involving youth, in-laws, business associates, fellow church members and neighbors may be salvaged. It's easier to write them off as disappointing. How-ever, it is much more gratifying to take the fragile components that make up any kind of human relationship and cement them together with understanding, patience and prayer, love and trust. Granted, the process may be tedious and time-consuming. But the secret ingredient to success, in many cases, is sheer determination.

In some disappointments the spirit of forgiveness appears as the distinguishing attribute which enables women to live serenely. So many women face disappointing actions on the part of their children. The problem is not new. The prodigal who took his portion of his father's goods and left home had a mother, too. She is not pictured by our Lord in his parable, but we can imagine the heartache, the tears, the grief she must have experienced as her son walked away and as the months passed without a word.

Today's prodigals cause similar grief. They move out into the hippie community. They run away. They turn to drugs and illicit sex. They break the law. Their marriages fail . . . and mothers weep.

The tendency to blame oneself, to harbor a sense of guilt, is no solution. Most would agree that a child usually reaches the "age of accountability" prior to the teen years. But some of us act as though we must assume total responsibility when a breach occurs. Has ever a mother lived who does not admit that, if she had it to do over again, she'd handle herself and her children a little differently? But the nursing of regrets can only be harmful. Surely this is not in harmony with the will of God for his children.

Instead, we must remember that with accountability comes a certain responsibility for wrong choices. In a seminar on "The New Morality and the Teen-ager," the lecturer said: "The child in your home, though he is the product of your love, is a distinct individual, and he may defy you and God."

It is a comfort, however, to remember that we have a loving, ready-to-forgive heavenly Father. Henry Ward Beecher has compared the graciousness of our God to that of a woman—"God pardons like a mother, who kisses the offence into everlasting forgetfulness." The grace of God, that *unmerited favor*, shown toward rebellious children is seen time and again in parents who "bend over backward" in an effort to help children who may have disappointed them.

In a college and career Bible study group, as we discussed the story of the prodigal son, two young people mentioned spontaneously the splendid relationship they each now enjoy with their parents, following a bout of rebellion and willfulness that took them away from home into dangerous and embarrassing situations. With a God-given love, parents can bridge the generation gap created by disappointment.

In some cases it is not forgiveness of others but the forgiving of oneself which is needed to bring about serenity. From wide experience in counseling, one minister notes that a big problem he has found among women is their inability to forgive themselves, even after they have consciously sought God's forgiveness for some breach of his will.

An attractive Christian woman in her forties confessed to her pastor that at one time she had been involved in an adulterous relationship. She had long since turned her back on the third party, had returned to her husband, and had earnestly sought his forgiveness and God's. But she could never quite forgive herself, and the experience had become a gnawing, haunting nightmare. Her pastor spent time in reassuring the woman of God's power to forgive and in reinforcing her confidence in his willingness to forgive. He helped her see she had not really accepted God's forgiveness until she forgave herself. He urged her to accept the fact, "What's done is done," to let bygones be bygones, to close the door on the incident, lock it, and throw away the key. The outcome of the conference was that she got rid of the burden of her guilt, at last turning her sin completely over to the Lord. It was a victory over the past, and her personality took on a new radiance.

In coping with disappointment, then, acceptance, a second-best dream, determination, and forgiveness may be indispensable to serenity. But, because I have seen the power of God working in the lives of so many who have found serenity in spite of disappointment, let me make one more suggestion. *Leave room for a miracle!*

Mary Farmer's story has convinced me. Her marriage began much like yours—with hopes, dreams, visions of a bright future. It was a wartime marriage, but the young have so much faith. Little did she dream that two months before their son was born, her husband's plane would be shot down by the Japanese over China. The official death message arrived the day their child was born.

Following her second marriage and soon after she had given birth to a second child, she walked into a famous hospital with leg pains which defied diagnosis. The decision to do exploratory spinal surgery resulted in paralysis—from her knees down. That same day her father died.

For six months Mary lived in a hospital. She had just begun to take five or six steps when one of her legs was broken in the process of the therapy. She has never walked since.

"Until I was twenty-two, the world was my oyster," she told me. She'd had a wholesome, normal childhood, had been a very popular young person—queen of all sorts of organizations, sweetheart of a boys' club, cheerleader, in the band, an accomplished tap dancer, a favorite date among the college athletes.

"Then, all of a sudden, wham! Things began happening to me, and each incident was dramatic, shocking, traumatic. The paralysis was the end and the beginning—of two distinctly different ways of life.

"I had this horrible pride, and it took me two years to accept the wheelchair. I hated it, I didn't want to be seen in it. I would go out in the car and sit outside my husband's place of business—but go in? Never! My shame was so intense. I wanted no one to see."

Finally, she resigned herself to life in a wheelchair and went on living, halfway. From her chair she managed to do the family laundry, to keep her house clean, to cook. "Some women would have copped out completely, but to feel honest I had to carry on there."

But she withdrew from the world outside. For years she would not even go onto her patio lest neighbors see her plight. For more than twenty years her world was extremely small.

Then, a Christian friend, her husband's business associate, insisted that her family attend a city-wide evangelistic crusade. Reluctantly, very reluctantly, she agreed. "I didn't want to go. But then I reasoned, nobody will know me."

But Someone did know her. That evening she gave God all the pieces of her broken life. High in the balcony of that coliseum, when the invitation was given, her young son tugged at his father's sleeve and said, "Daddy, I want to go."

"I did, too," Mary said. "The divine call was so urgent!" The final hymn was coming to a close as the whole family moved out, wheelchair and all, for what looked like an impossible trek down to where the ministers stood waiting.

I did not know her before this happened. I only know what I see—a serene and lovely woman worshiping with her family regularly in our church. But friends tell me they have seen a miracle, and I, hearing, find myself believing more deeply in the power of God to transform lives broken by disappointment.

As church librarian, Mary has been responsible for setting up a well-organized and most attractive library. During Sunday School she teaches young teen-agers. For two years now she has directed a junior high department in Vacation Bible School.

Last winter she received still another blow. Doctors discovered a malignancy and there was extensive surgery. A lesser person would have said, "This is it!" but Mary Farmer bounced back and weeks later was in charge of hosting an area library clinic in her church.

"Sometimes it seems I sit around and wonder what's going to happen next," she laughed as we talked together. "But I know all of this has made me more of a person. I've been able to roll with the punches very well. Oh, I have my upsets but how I love life! It isn't really normal to accept life like this. Some great people in the Lord have prayed for me, and he has given me a strong mind, intestinal fortitude, and the 'something extra' necessary for living around disappointment."

The list of disappointments that plague man and woman are long as life itself. Many are nursed and fed by constant self-concern and self-pity. They can destroy a person. Or they can be dealt with, managed.

When hope is blighted, plans are thwarted, dreams denied, try to get the problem out of the emotional realm and examine it objectively, intellectually, rationally. Is your disappointment premature? Have you allowed enough time for your hope to materialize? Maybe you're just discouraged and should not grant the stamp of finality to the situation yet. What can you do about it?

Was it a valid expectation in the first place? Have you done your part in bringing it to reality? If you did slip up somewhere, don't harbor regrets or guilt. Ask God's forgiveness, if you have disappointed him, and then forgive yourself. Was your hope self-centered? Was it actually best for you and all concerned?

Accept failure when it's final. Make a new appointment with hope. Determine what you can salvage from the experience. If you can't have a full loaf, you may have to settle for a half. Dream a possible dream.

And remember, "God can do wonders with a broken heart if you give him all the pieces." Leave room for a miracle!

When Your Problem Is Indecision

"Take charge of your life, you
can do what you will with it."
—Plato

"I wonder sometimes what I should do," a little red-haired woman from Arizona, the mother of two small children, said to me. "I go to church, and the emphasis is on the urgency of my homemaking, parent task. I return home to try harder to be a better homemaker and mother. Again I go, and the cry is for women to take responsibility for the missions tasks of the church. I add to my volunteer load additional duties outlined by the church.

"Again I go, and the point is plainly made that we Christians aren't doing enough—'do more, do more!' I leave feeling guilty because the pastor says, 'God needs more workers!'

"I return to a house left cluttered from a busy day of church work, to a family fretful because of the disorder.

"Sometimes I wonder. . . . How do I find the answers? *Does the God of peace have any answers for the conscientious Christian woman faced with innumerable choices of good?*"

Torn between religious duty and home responsibilities, this woman has expressed just one facet of the role uncertainty so common among women today.

Does the God of peace have any answers? Must Christian women live lives doomed to an uncomfortable, naggingly uncertain discipleship?

The little mother from Arizona is not alone in her dilemma. A dedicated children's worker on her way to lead a conference in a nearby church expressed frustration because she could not be present for the activity scheduled in her own church that evening. How sad when a competent Christian in demand outside her local church feels a sense of guilt—and uncertainty about the reaction of other Christians!—when she is called upon to serve elsewhere. Or, when one doing a good job in one post feels guilt because she has to say no to another responsibility.

A sweet-faced woman with a mentally retarded son whom she dares not leave alone more than an hour or two at most tearfully expressed her frustration following a devotional urging women to "put Christ first" in their lives. My heart went out to her as I tried to help her know there's more to loyalty than committee-ing for Christ. But a great many people, it seems, think "church work" when they hear "Christ." The "J-O-Y" idea, "Jesus first, Others second, Yourself last," sounds great, but actually how does one "put Christ first" without serving others in the process, except in worship? Don't those "others" include the persons nearest and dearest to us?

Conflict arises and uncertainty creeps in when one's husband is not equally interested and involved in the work of the church. A highly reliable youth worker sought her pastor's help in reaching a decision when her husband's desires conflicted with her church interests. A red-letter day was coming up in the Sunday School, the very weekend her husband wanted her to accompany him on a business trip to a well-known resort. Pulled between the two, she couldn't bring herself to say yes to her husband. Her pastor said, "Go with him! Your first duty is to your husband!" Amazingly, the pastor relates, not long afterward the husband became heavily involved in the life of the church right along with his wife.

Now, this pastor was not saying a woman should devote her complete life to a backsliding husband to the neglect of her church responsibilities. But his counsel was based on the wisdom that a man must know of his wife's deep respect and love and must be assured he does not have a rival in her church.

I have seen women whose husbands were openly resentful of their wives' participations in church life manage, through prayer and loving consideration, to find ways of service which did not antagonize their mates. Interest has a way of compounding interest, and sometimes these husbands have found their way to God through the gentle, patient leading of their wives. No doubt the wife's testimony of genuine love for husband as well as for the Lord has had its effect.

I have had my own uncertainties about "religious duty." At missions meetings the needs of persons who are not immediate prospects for my church are made plain; aged people needing visits, help needed with a language group in an inner-city church, transportation needed for the infirm. At other meetings, the call is to visit prospects for the church: persons who are not believers, inactive church members. The phone rings: "Will I serve? Will I speak? Can I help?" I pick up the daily paper and read pleas for volunteers for at least fifty-seven varieties of community services. Looking out my window, I catch a glimpse of a lonely neighbor. I think of my family: a husband whose companionship I enjoy, who relies upon me even as I do upon him. Children—grown now—deserving my letters of love and interest and confidence. My favorite senior citizen, Mother, far away, living alone.

What's a woman to do when she is faced with such countless choices—all good? Some of them are not "I will or I won't" matters. More of them are "How much?" questions.

She is fortunate if she can determine her "major" and her "minors." There is serenity in the knowledge that she cannot possibly major in everything. Her major may be youth work at church or her growing family. It may be music, or it may be assisting her husband in his work. It may be a career in which she believes, or it may be political activity.

An intense woman I know has majored for years in the private morning preschool which she operates. She has not neglected her family; she has been very active in her church. And her "minors"! She has such a diversity of interests and a keen desire to explore them. Out-of-town friends ask smilingly, "What's Helen into these days?" One year it was a Japanese garden complete with waterfall. Another, sewing lingerie. Last time I saw her she was decoupaging everything in sight. And now I understand she is an avid participant in youth evangelism. But none of these interests have interfered with the "major" she chose years ago when she began her work with little children.

C. A. Stoddards once said: "When we can say 'no,' not only to things which are wrong and sinful, but also to things pleasant, profitable, and good *which would hinder and clog our grand duties and our chief work,* we shall understand more fully what life is worth, and how to make the most of it."

The apostle Paul indicated the need for careful choices: "My prayer for you is that your love may grow ever richer and richer in knowledge of every kind, and may thus bring you the gift of true discrimination." God's Word is filled with promises to grant wisdom, which is, after all, the priceless gift of true discrimination. What a serenity we can experience when we know we have chosen well!

Sometimes choosing the "more excellent" involves denying ourselves immediate pleasure and profit in favor of a long-term gain. But when one has a sense of having God's wholehearted approval, how gratifying it can be.

Today I talked with one of the most gracious and selfless Christian women I've ever known. She said no to the state-level position of service in our missions organization about which I was calling. I know it was work she considered pleasant, profitable, and good, for rather than resigning in the spring when her daughter became ill she had taken a leave of absence, hoping to resume her responsibilities a little later on. But she said no in favor of her "grand duty and chief work"—as mother and wife. Right now her family needed her in new ways which would have conflicted with this work.

It hurts me to hear women criticizing their sisters who are unable to put in as many hours at the church as some others. Particularly when they may be rendering a greater service through their acts of love to the children, the youth, the men—and sometimes the senior citizens—in their homes.

I cannot recall all the dedicated Christian women I've known who have said no to certain "sacred" duties in favor of their grand duty and chief work—their careers. But I am sympathetic when I know these women see their total life as service to the Lord. And until a woman gets the dimensional impact of her total life as being "Christian," she will continually have difficulty finding serenity in the midst of her many roles.

Actually, are we any less our heavenly Father's child when we are getting dinner for our family, or manning a school lunchroom, than when we are teaching a Bible class or staffing the church nursery? Or do we merely pacify ourselves by thinking we have served our Master only in church-related, church-directed tasks? Do we view life as a patchwork quilt of activities, the solid colors "sacred," the calico ones "secular?" Or do we see it as a length of a single fabric (the selvage with the manufacturer's trademark, "Christian"), the whole piece revealing the pattern and the quality of his workmanship in our lives?

We do not have to be naggingly uncertain about our role as Christian women. If we can get rid of the patchwork notion, we will be able to live much more serenely. The design of our life is a flowing one, diverse yet unified by the fact of *whose we are.* In every situation we are Christ's. This is the one stabilizing, controlling fact of our life which can give assurance and certainty to our decisions.

Time use is one of the ever present uncertainties with which women must deal, especially if they are full-time homemakers with a margin of leisure. Take, for example, one of those rare days when nothing specific is scheduled. Now's a time to choose. But little duties pop through the subconscious like punches on a computer card. Big projects make their claims. Weekly responsibilities, present themselves. Often without conscious awareness of what is going on, we make our decisions. Sometimes one after another, in series; again, one at a time. Some days we wander indecisively, wondering at day's end why we've absolutely nothing to show for the hours gone by.

On what basis can a Christian woman make wise decisions about time use? First, she can claim the promise of God to give wisdom: "If any of you lack it, ask me, I'll give it to you generously, and I won't scold you for asking." Then she might ask herself such questions as:

- Is someone relying on me for something? Is it a legitimate need? How can I best fulfil it?

- What can I do to make life easier, more pleasant, and profitable for someone close to me?
- Is there someone who needs what I can offer in services and goods? Am I in a position to meet this need at this point in my life? Would it be worthwhile and advisable to make arrangements which would permit me to meet this need?
- How am I utilizing and/or conserving my God-given talents and abilities?
- What do I personally need to do if I am to be a whole person, useful to God and others?
- Is it possible that I actually need to be idle for a while?
- How much time do I waste each day and in what ways?
- What does the Holy Spirit seem to be saying to me about the use of my time today?

Some years ago a man who made a study of serenity said, "Preoccupation with trivialities fills the lives of myriads of men and women who never become aware that nothing is more exhausting and irritating or does more harm to the cause of serenity than the empty feeling at the end of a wasted day."

I would agree—unless one has wasted a day on purpose. Hugh Downs, for nine years host to N.B.C.'s "Today Show," says he's learned it's a good idea to goof off sometimes. Brought up believing time should never be squandered, he felt every moment should be filled with "meaningful activity." Fortunately, though, he outgrew his sense of guilt and he said in a *Look* magazine interview: "I now allow what I call my sense of responsibility to atrophy somewhat. I rationalize that if it is necessary for me to squander and waste a percentage of my time in order to avoid derailment, then that is not squandered or wasted." It is a blessed gift to be able to turn off the tensions and pressures, like a distasteful television program, and turn to nothing, if one wishes, or to whatever is restful and refreshing to the spirit, however inconsequential.

*   *   *

Surely Shakespeare, comparing life to a drama with its cast of actors, did not envision the diversified roles women would be permitted to play in the twentieth century. Certainly my grandmother, who gave birth to fifteen children, never dreamed of the choices women today must make in a lifetime. She never had to decide whether or not to have children, and how many. What kind of birth control to practice. Whether to stay home and be a full-time mother or go out into the business world in competition with the opposite sex. Whether to stick it out with Grandpa when the going got tough or to declare her independence from him. Or what to do with her leisure time.

It isn't easy, Grandma! Granted, you had a hard life, but woman's liberation from your kind of life has bred a new strain of stresses, producing an enormous frustration among women.

The feminine malaise of "role uncertainty" is very real. Listen to a male's—Morton M. Hunt—description of our ailment: "The American woman is, in sum, a set of odds and ends of her own history, worked into the strange fabric of her new contemporary self. She is something of a lover and mistress, something of a housewife and mother, something of a success-oriented emancipated woman; she is a bit of a courtesan, of an intellectual, of the biblical good wife, and of a handful of other leftovers of time, all assembled upon the canvas of her present days and ways. She may be man's lover, his mate, or his rival—or something of each, blended and entangled in any one of a score of ways. History has given her the precedent for each of these aspects of her being, but it has never told her how to be all of them at once; this is her problem today, and her continuing quest."

I like to think we Christian women are different. But we too are American women, shaped far more than we realize by an educational system that treats boys and girls equally and by an economy that so far has fallen short in this respect. Shaped too, subconsciously, by the abnormal feminine caricatures contrived by Madison Avenue and Hollywood. Enough to make us uncertain!

The forces which have driven more than thirty-one million American women into jobs beyond the home have probably contributed most of all to our uncertainty. For the tradition that woman's place is in the home continues to hold sway, even when the home has been rapidly emptied by early marriage and family planning. And despite the electrical servants and mass production which have taken over most of the homemaking tasks.

Following publication of *The Christian Woman in the Working World,* one reader wrote, "I can count on one hand the women I know who have never worked. Those who no longer do seem to keep playing with the idea of gainful employment. Unfortunately, many of them may have to find a job if inflation continues." Another wrote, "Too long we have felt guilty about working. I still will agree that if a mother can stay at home—that makes it another story."

The uncertainty working mothers experience is probably due to the fact that women have difficulty separating their parent-role from their occupational role. Marriage, home, and family are integral parts of their lives. Women seldom can dissociate themselves from their role as wives and homemakers, regardless of the position they hold in the business and professional world.

This built-in sense of responsibility is not all bad, either. For while technology has taken care of so many of the tasks that were the drudgery of woman's life for centuries, nothing has yet replaced the caring touch of a woman for her family, and a mother knows it.

She knows no technological achievement will ever be able to nurture small boys and girls into secure, happy, useful individuals. Man will never invent a machine which will deliver child-size doses of affection, acceptance, approval, and appreciation.

Many mothers seem to know instinctively that a child needs what Dr. Tournier calls a "place"—a genuine community into which he can really fit and to which he can return, if only in a spiritual sense later on. They will agree with him that "the ideal place for the child is the family." They know the quality of the home-place depends so much upon the mother at its heart.

Unfortunately, all mothers do not have a choice. The rising numbers of divorcées and the growing numbers of unwed mothers who keep their young have helped bring the total number of families where women are the head of the house and sole support of the family to five million. These mothers do not have a choice.

Others are victims of those decisions requiring a monthly response in dollars and cents. Some of these decisions are minor ones, but they can add up to the necessity for two incomes.

The capable young modern knows all about the "just a housewife" syndrome. She doesn't want to be a "mom" type, living vicariously through her youngsters. She's seen the unhappy female who demands too much of her marriage simply because she doesn't have anything else to occupy her boredom-dulled mind.

While she recognizes the urgency for stable homes in our fast-moving world, she feels she must have some diversion from dishes, debts, diapers, and the conversational level of a four-year-old. And if debt is a part of the problem, making money seems logical. Most of all, though, she experiences the need for recognition and appreciation.

But, wait a minute; what about the kids?

Most Christian women will agree with Billy Graham that a woman's first responsibility is that of wife and mother. But for some there remains yet the nagging uncertainty: "Must the answer be either homemaking or employment? Or can I handle both effectively?"

Some who have studied the problems of the employed mother say it is the quality of time a mother gives her children rather than the quantity which is more important. Some studies have shown that children of working mothers fare better than those who want to work but who stay home out of a sense of duty.

But woman after woman who comes home jaded and weary from a day at a typewriter, or with feet aching from an eight-hour stint on a hospital floor, or from six or seven hours of attempting to cope with a classroom full of youngsters knows quality of care often suffers. And I shudder to think what the four-day, forty-hour week may do to mothers and their young! Can three days with the children make up for the four when they'll scarcely see Mom? Do children's needs come in three-day parcels?

It takes a certain quantity of time to look after children and to provide a security from which they can go forth always assured of a "place." Nor is it only the very young children who need their mothers! Teen-agers need them terribly these days.

Recent statistics indicate one fourth of all wives with children under three, one third of those with children under five, and half the mothers of school-age children are employed. Could these notable statistics relate in any way to the incidence of runaways, drug dependents, and other juveniles in trouble throughout America? What about findings that the peers of our youth have more influence upon them than parents and teachers?

The most recent White House Conference on Children and Youth sounded a morbid note in its report to the President. "America's families and their children are in trouble, trouble so deep and pervasive as to threaten the future of the nation. The source of the trouble is nothing less than a national neglect of children and those primarily engaged in their care—America's parents. . . ."

Decisions! Should Mother, or shouldn't she, work outside the home? Let's try rewording that question. Isn't there some way a mother could work just part of the time if she chooses and still have time and energy left to fulfil her home responsibilities?

The decision between homemaking versus career does not necessarily have to be an either-or situation. I strongly agree with a widely circulated women's magazine which recently queried, "Who says the thirty-five hour week is sacred?" Today many mothers are successfully marketing their skills on *their* terms. They are bargaining for flexible hours which permit them to be at home when their children are home. Half-day teachers, part-time clerical workers, beauticians, medical assistants, salespeople, and, more and more, women with highly specialized skills and administrative ability, are finding part-time niches in the working world. Prejudice toward the part-timer is lessening. In some organizations status and seniority are not affected when a woman takes an extended leave or goes to part-time for the sake of her family. Employers are often startled to discover they are getting more for their money from part-timers.

A New York City employment agency contends most jobs can be done in a five-hour day, anyway—not a bad workday at all for a healthy, well-organized mother. So what if she does take home 30 percent less pay? Wouldn't it be worth it for the sake of the kids?

It is strange, isn't it, that nearly 50 percent of all mothers had entered the labor market before an effective way of combining motherhood with outside employment ever occurred to us? Creative solutions are coming about as concerned women follow a cardinal rule in problem-solving, "juggling the elements." Until recently, our mental set indicated employment meant a forty or thirty-five hour week. That was that! Until the light gradually broke through our rigid thinking and revealed more than one way to get a job done!

Of course, the busy, contented mother should not jump into her little car and run for the nearest part-time job upon reading this! Some women make better homemakers and mothers than anything else. Some would be miserable trying to handle anything more than their homes and families. Some have learned to value their bit of leisure. Some husbands would say an unequivocal "Never" to the idea.

Many women find great satisfaction in their work as homemakers and look upon their freedom to give themselves unreservedly to that task as a blessing. They seem to have an innate awareness of the value to both man and child of a woman's tender interest and unfailing support. They realize the contribution a pleasant, orderly, unhurried, serene atmosphere in the home can make to the lives of husbands and children. They are conscious of the rippling influence for good that moves out from a strong and creative home into the community and the world. They feel sufficiently needed and rewarded in making such a home. Some who may experience strong urges to assert their abilities in other areas have realized that in today's world a woman's life lasts far beyond the mothering years, and there's time enough for that in the future.

Each of us is unique, and our home responsibilities and relationships are highly diversified. So—to each her own! The decision is highly personal, and it should, of course, be mutually agreed upon by husband and wife. And remember, what may be a "right" decision now will probably need reevaluation later on as your role in your "original" family drama changes.

*   *   *

Decisions! Decisions! Decisions!

Life offers more choices than a seed catalog on a late winter evening. Sometimes we feel like crying out: "Lord, it would have been a whole lot simpler if you'd made things just black-and-white, cut-and-dried, with not so many choices!"

You may be faced with a decision far removed from the three I've discussed which cause so much uncertainty in women's lives. Yours may be a major decision (And a minor decision, like surgery, seems major when it's happening to you!). Let's look at what's involved in sound decision-making.

Each woman brings certain individual factors to her problem-solving. There is the mental set with which we approach our problem. Conventional wisdom and opinions become a part of us and we tend to bring these to our problems first of all. Also, we may bring a rigidity of thinking which causes us to say "I can't" or "I won't" or "I'm afraid to," even before we think through the problem. Such foregone conclusions must be set aside in favor of a fresh look at our situation. This is why it is often helpful to discuss difficult problems with an outsider who may help us consider aspects which otherwise might escape our notice.

Then, we bring past experience to bear upon our problems. What hasn't worked previously, we reject almost automatically. Relevant past experience is likely to play a major role in the solution, that is, unless it blinds us. What others have told us and what we have read enter the picture.

Our personal context affects our decision. The fact that we are Junior's mother or Joe's wife can make it difficult to see problems involving them in a true light.

The degree of stress under which we must make a decision affects our problem-solving ability. When livelihood, reputation, or our future are threatened or when we have suffered shock, it is difficult to make complex decisions. This is why widows are counseled to delay decision-making immediately following their bereavement.

One's sense of personal worth affects the ability to decide. Self-respect is like a personal safety zone which protects us from fear of what others may think of our choice. When we believe in our own dignity and worth, we do not fear so much the possibility of a mistake. And we must remember nobody is always 100 percent right. We're all entitled to a few mistakes in a lifetime. And, to not decide because we're fearful is to do nothing.

Here are five steps which may help you in reaching your decision:

1. *State the problem and define your goal.*

Remember a problem well defined is half solved. A woman must not overstep herself, however! One woman recounted the year her husband's corporation literally dumped her, along with furniture and youngsters, into a new city and promptly sent her husband out of town, leaving her with dozens of decisions. Upon his return, as she was bringing him up to date on family doings, he commented dryly, "My, you've become awfully independent lately!" She pointed out a wife must sense where to draw the lines between decisions which are "his," "hers," and "ours." "I had to learn," she said, "to make necessary decisions when my husband was away, then seek, accept, and respect his judgment on those he wishes to participate in when he's available. I've found our joint decisions simpler if I do some footwork in exploring alternatives in advance." And, speaking of alternatives, that's the second step.

2. *Explore the alternatives.*

Here, from Ralph Carmichael's folk musical, "Tell It Like It Is," is the idea:

> Answers are not easy comin'
> Even to a full time mind.
> Part time searchin' easy goin'
> Make the answers hard to find.
> Truth is like a sphere shaped object
> More than just one simple side.
> Wait till all the facts assemble
> Ponder some and then decide.[1]

Looking at others' decision, we rarely think of their alternatives. But imagine, if you will, the alternatives behind the decisions of Esther, Ruth, the widow with the two mites, the woman with the alabaster box of ointment. There is so much more than one simple alternative!

3. *"Ponder some" and then decide.*

Snap decisions are not always wise ones. Hastily formulated, inadequate decisions sometimes have to be lived with for a long time. And some decisions chain-react like a row of dominoes laid low by the barest touch. Better to look before you leap. Allow a time lapse after your first approach to a knotty problem. Sleep on it. Take a second look before firming up your decision. You may find you've failed to consider some obscure aspect of the problem that will affect your decision. This pondering time allows you to "put two and two together" and to gain insight into the total situation. This is the time when you may experience inspiration or illumination.

Peter Drucker, in *The Effective Executive,* writes, "Decisions almost make themselves when specifications have been thought through, alternatives explored, risks and gains weighed. . . ." But, he notes, the effective decision-maker does not delay too long—a few days, at most a few weeks.

4. *Put the decision into effect.*

This is the most time-consuming step, but Mr. Drucker says: "Unless a decision 'has degenerated into work' it is not a decision; it is at best a good intention." A classic feminine example: dieting! A classic biblical example: the prodigal son, who came to himself, saw himself, made a decision, and "arose and came unto his father." When a positive decision is reached and one begins to put it into effect, a kind of serenity pervades the life. Relief, calmness, composure come when at last the mind is "made up."

5. *Evaluate your action.*

Check the results against your expectations. Be prepared to adapt, adjust, modify, or rescind your action if these are indicated. Sometimes we hide our heads in the sand, so to speak, lest we discover we need to rethink a matter and chart a new course. Creative living

requires continual evaluation of our actions, or we fall into compla-
cency and ineffectiveness.

Keep in mind, some situations don't require a decision. Occasionally, the best action we can take is to do nothing. But when a situation
is likely to worsen, decisions are imperative.

Even as we utilize the powers within us—to state the problem, to
evaluate alternatives, to ponder, and to act; as we utilize available
resources outside ourselves—the counsel of wise friends, information
agencies, and books—let us never forget there is yet another source
to which we can turn for effective decision-making.

God waits for his children, lacking wisdom, to turn to him with
their problems. If we are open and honest with him, the Holy Spirit
will call to our minds counsel from God's Word which will provide
a background of wisdom. He will reprove us if we are on the wrong
track. And, as so many Christians affirm, he has strange ways of
leading us along paths which we may never have dreamed of nor
planned on taking.

The value of a decision to follow Jesus Christ cannot be emphasized
too strongly. This basic decision can eliminate innumerable little
uncertainties. The decision in favor of a life of Christian discipleship
is a decision in favor of a valid standard. A point of reference is
established by which all alternatives may safely be measured. A sound
value system is adopted. Right and wrong activities are more easily
sorted. Week-to-week decisions about church attendance, service in
his name, and giving are simplified. The serious Christian disciple is
automatically a goal-oriented, goal-striving individual.

Actually we are the sum of our choices. I like the way Rona Jaffe
put it in *The Best of Everything:* "Many people look back and say,
this was the day that changed my life. They are never wholly right.
The day you choose one college instead of another, or decide not to
go to college at all, the day you take one job instead of another because
you cannot wait, the day you meet someone you later love—all are
days that lead to change, but none of them are decisive because *the
choice itself is the unconscious product of days that have gone before.*"

To live serenely then is to live each day in such a way that we need not fear the future and its inherent decisions. When we've made today's decisions carefully and we've done what we could to effect them, let's not fret ourselves further.

Remember the advice on the package of tulip bulbs! "Just put 'em in the ground and walk away whistling!"

7
Handling Feminine Anxieties

"It ain't no use putting up your
umbrella 'til it rains."
—Alice Hegan Rice

Ever since Eve, women have lived with anxieties. Imagine Eve's anxiety as she followed Adam out of the Garden. Would they be able to manage out there? Her sense of guilt, added to the dread of a move into a strange environment, was probably complicated by a fear common to women even in a more enlightened age—pregnancy. What was going on inside her body? Her marriage was beset with conflict over recent events. Who was to blame? And what could she do about it now? Adam would scarcely speak to her when she tried to make excuse. And, as always with women, there was dinner to get, and not only nothing in the house to set before her husband, but no house! And, worry of worries, that animal skin—all she had to put on!

Anxiety had entered the world, and so anxiety fell upon all women. While man has helped us conquer our fears—of food spoilage, of most illnesses, of cold and heat, and of darkness—multitudes of others have cropped up to take their place.

Over tousled heads of tiny sons, women gaze upon such horrors of war as mothers of the past never imagined. They view the destructiveness of drugs. Constantly they are reminded of the dread "seven danger signals." What happened to a streetwalker in Hoboken reaches them in living color. The complicated narratives of lives marred by sin feed their imaginations when the news reports are finished. And all about, there are the Joneses.

Let me use the terms "fear" and "anxiety" almost interchangeably for this discussion. For, as Paul Tillich says in *The Courage to Be,* "fear and anxiety are distinguished but not separated." Fear is "a feeling of alarm or disquiet caused by the expectation of danger, pain, disaster, or the like." Fear is not all bad, for it alerts the mind to action when danger is approaching. Psychologists refer to fear as a reaction to danger that is real, specific, and from an outside cause.

Anxiety is "the painful feeling of not being able to deal with the threat of a special situation," according to Tillich. It may be a reaction to unknown, vague threats from within. Because it has no object to which it may react, it is characterized by a sense of helplessness.

The mother with the young son watches clips from the drug scene across the nation and experiences fear—a feeling of alarm that her son might someday become involved. At the same time she feels anxiety—a helplessness at her inability to cope with the problem. And she may begin to worry, becoming greatly agitated mentally. She could become obsessed, unreasoning, and suspicious, and at this point she would be in need of professional help.

The causes underlying anxiety are legion, but let's examine three areas of anxiety which seem to plague women in particular: anxiety for personal safety, the anxieties of parenthood, and anxiety over physical change. Actually, getting them out into the open is a beginning place for conquest.

Scarcely a woman alive has not known, at some time or another, the anxiety of being alone without the protection of a male companion.

A competent young secretary asked me to say something about this kind of anxiety. "Jerry works late, you know," she said, "and since we moved into a big house with a basement, I'm nearly ill with fear each evening. Just recently, there was a burglary only a couple of homes away. When I've checked and double-checked all the windows and doors, I go and hide in the bathroom (the only room with no windows). Many times I leave an hour early to go pick him up and sit waiting in the locked car, rather than stay in that house by myself."

This young woman is not alone in her concern. A widow, who prior to her husband's death had been active in numerous evening activities, describes her fear at going into her house alone at night. An executive's wife says she avoids going out alone in the evenings, as even the short well-lighted distance between the open parking area and her townhouse is potentially dangerous. A leader of a women's organization notes that numbers of groups in cities have discontinued evening meetings because of incidents of violence in the streets. Interest in classes in self-defense is further evidence of the widespread anxiety among women for their safety.

With the numbers of would-be molesters, muggers, and obscene telephone callers on the increase and with safe neighborhoods few and far between, much of our concern for personal safety is justifiable.

Now, if you're expecting me to give only a "religious" solution to this kind of anxiety, you'll be disappointed. I believe God expects us to blend available resources for protection with a good-sized portion of trust in his protecting care. He didn't give us common sense and a drive for self-protection for nothing. I've observed that most people who say they "turn things over to the Lord" don't often mention the "meanwhiles" of their efforts. They don't sit around doing nothing.

In a recent article in *Today's Health,* Duane Valentry suggests that the first place to begin in maintaining personal safety is in the way we dress and act. He points out that tight, skimpy clothing and provocative behavior are an invitation to trouble. Even innocent familiarities with strangers may be a prelude to crime.

Go ahead and be leery, Mr. Valentry advises. Light your house and yard well. When arriving home in the evening, shine your headlights on the house and leave them on until you have opened the door. Inside, make use of those lights and locks. Peepholes on the front door and chain bolts are not just for "fraidy-cats." They are sensible protection. Police phone numbers plainly posted near telephones are added insurance against anxiety. Use them if you suspect trouble.

Precautions in driving alone, especially at night, are advised. Keep a full tank of gas and use those door locks and the windows. The *Today's Health* article tells the woman with car trouble to put up the hood and trunk and remain inside the car with windows up. Then, if a lone man approaches with an offer to help, stay inside and ask him to send help back.

Advertising one's aloneness is one kind of advertising that does not pay. A recent widow, on receiving a call asking for her husband, bravely followed a sensible rule many women observe, that of never telling strange callers they are alone. Valentry says one woman answers such a question with: "Just a minute, please. I'll call my brother the fighter." Often women alone list their initials rather than their given names in phone directories to lessen the likelihood of obscene or curious calls. A single woman flaunts a man's hat in the back of her car. A married woman whose husband is an avid hunter leaves a pair of boots on the doorstep when he is away.

As for weapons, authorities say both guns and tear gas can be dangerous, depending upon the type of weapon, the type of woman using it, her skill at handling it, and her legal knowledge of when to use a weapon. In most places it is illegal to carry a weapon. But, if it is necessary for a woman to walk alone in dark or deserted areas, she might consider carrying one of the pocket alarms now on the market.

Experts tell women fearful of their personal safety to keep in mind their God-given resources—their scream (a hysterical blood-curdling scream is a woman's best weapon); their legs (for running); their teeth (for biting); and their fingernails (for scratching). Fifty thousand American women reportedly have been developing their natural resources through the study of judo! We are told just flashing a membership card in the judo association will put a man to flight in terror. But if it's money he's after, don't resist. Your life is more valuable.

However, even when one is satisfied that she has taken adequate precautionary measures in making her residence secure and in developing habits which discourage trouble, there may yet be mental habits which must be changed if she is to enjoy serenity.

First, realize that anxiety which puts you on guard against trouble is good but that over-anxiety does nothing but damage the personality of the worrier. When you've acted sensibly to prevent trouble, relax and enjoy life. The woman who lives confidently is much better prepared to act wisely should an emergency arise.

Then, practice thought control. At a time in my life when I was regularly lying awake with anxiety, there was a specific point at which

I realized: This is ridiculous. I've got to get hold of myself. From that moment I was able to sleep, even under circumstances which might have made me anxious, had I permitted them to. Refuse to allow your mind to dwell on the dangerous. Control that imagination. Regulate your thinking by shutting away the hair-raising story or picture which may have its adverse aftereffects. "Whatsoever things are of good report, . . ." think on *those* things. Stimulate your thinking on a variety of subjects by reading, chatting, shopping, walking. Don't let your mind get hung up, like a broken record, on remote possibilities. Discard the "record"; replace it with fresh thoughts.

Don't hoard your fears. Get them out into the open. Make a list, if you wish; it's amazing how getting a problem into black-and-white can give perspective. Bringing your fears without apology to the light of another's viewpoint can help them to vanish. By all means, discuss your fears with your husband, with a friend, or with a counselor. "True courage," someone has said, "begins with the admission of anxiety."

If you live alone, look about you at all the other women who do so, in safety. Talk with some whom you admire for their resourcefulness and self-confidence.

Put your trust in God. Medical specialists writing in a recent book on the problem of anxiety said, "It appears as though the loss of a profound religious faith has helped open the door to anxiety for many." Believe in the Lord, thy keeper, who never slumbers or sleeps. Believe that his eye is on the sparrow, and he's watching over you. Be like the little woman who said: "Every night I say my prayers and then I remember 'ow the parson told us God is always watching, so I go to sleep. After all, there's no need for two of us to lie awake."

A wise friend reminded me that true serenity is a product of security. Describing the rabbit in his backyard, he noted that this wild creature, in the midst of a modern city, is as calm as though he were in the middle of a ten-acre field all to himself. "Maybe it's because there's a clump of poppy plants in the middle of the yard in which he has a hiding place. Or maybe it's because he's made so that he trusts the hiding place to protect him.

"The wild creature by instinct knows to trust his hiding place. The Christian by choice must trust in God as his refuge."

A missionary to Vietnam described her all-enveloping fear as she lay with her family under mattresses in a hallway during a severe military attack. With rockets exploding all around her, she said she found it impossible to communicate peace and courage to her children. That is, until she pulled herself together and prayed, "O Lord, thou who hast put us here to serve thee in this place, we now commit ourselves unto thee." She said, "With that prayer instant peace and calm came over me." This was no "heavenly bosom" kind of trust that does nothing in face of danger. Remember the mattresses! But it was an honest admission on her part that in that moment she desperately needed a refuge beyond human possibility. God tells us repeatedly that he is just that, a refuge and a fortress for those who turn to him in their moments of extremity.

Finally, combat your anxieties over your personal safety in our violent society by thanking God every morning for his watchcare over you. With repeated expressions of gratitude, your trust and dependence upon him will grow. And your anxieties will proportionately diminish.

To discuss anxiety among women without touching upon the parental concerns for youth growing up amid the pressures of our times would be to ignore a vital problem affecting serenity.

The black shadow of the drug menace hangs over the nation, and no home with youngsters is exempt from anxiety lest it too might be affected. The shadow has already touched too many homes, and mothers are ill from anxiety for their young. In some cases, the trouble has been comparatively minor. But, as one mother whose son had experimented with a small amount of LSD said, "I don't know whether I can live with this fear or not."

Complicating the scene are thousands of youthful runaways who leave anxious parents behind. The numbers are so large that community agencies say they cannot begin to offer effective assistance in locating all who are reported to them. More recently, I am told, fewer youngsters are running away from home, but many continue to reject their parents and are moving in with families of friends.

A Christian mother living in a northern city expressed the anxieties of so many parents of dating teen-agers. "We *can't* always know who they're with! Nor where they are at 10 P.M. Back when I was dating, my folks knew everyone in town. They knew the families of the boys I dated. Places to go on a date were so limited, they could pretty well keep up with us. But today—so the kids can't get into the bowling lanes they'd planned on. There are dozens of choices for other entertainment. They can be all the way across the city in minutes. And handy as phones are, and much as our teen-agers hang on to them at home, they forget there is such a thing when plans are changed.

"We move so often (uprooted, you know!) we scarcely know anyone in the community. We have to trust our sons and daughters to choose their companions, and relationships frequently have deepened before we find out much about them."

Add to these worries, concerns for the quality of education your child is receiving, plus the pros and cons about bussing. And the strange cults of mystical orientation many youth are exploring. Throw in a generous helping of anxiety over illicit sex. One college student said, "Any mother who doesn't worry about premarital sex has to be blind!"

Some authorities, with the wisdom of hindsight rather than foresight, feel we parents have become anxious too late. Until the plague of marijuana, hard drugs, alcohol, sex before marriage, and delinquency strikes the homes of friends, we tend to go our merry way, anxious about other matters.

So maybe the beginnings of anxiety we are seeing in quite young parents is good. It is good if it causes them to take a long, hard look at child-rearing practices. If it causes them to realize that parenthood and the processes of communication between parent and child are time-consuming, requiring more than the leftovers of a parent's interest. If it helps them see that work-work-work and too little rest are sometimes responsible for "pushaway children."

I talked with Jim Groen, executive director of Denver Area Youth for Christ, a man who has done an outstanding work with youth and parents of troubled youth as well.

He said, "I feel it most urgent that the anxious parent examine his own life for inconsistencies. My counseling experience indicates eight out of every ten young people I talk with are reacting to an adult problem or inconsistency in the home. Parents need to examine their lives to see if they are of a quality that would motivate a child to good behavior. They must face up to the question, 'Are we living by a double standard—one for us, one for our young?' "

Commenting on the fact that 25 percent of our children and youth are being raised by parents other than their own or by institutions, he noted: "Two essentials vital to a child's proper development are warmly firm parents who admire each other and who set an example youth can follow during the breakaway years; and the opportunity for the youth to emerge as a distinct, unique personality."

He calls for a return to firm discipline, beginning with the very young, "a unity between parents, respect, trust, and training all backed by example, administered in love, consistency, and honesty." He says children must be encouraged to face reality, to take responsibility for their actions.

Questioned about parental anxiety when a youngster is on drugs, he said: "Drug use is a symptom of deeper problems. While we may hate the act, we must never stop loving our child. Too often, parents get so uptight they alienate themselves from their son or daughter. At a time when patience and love are so direly needed. . . .

"But," he believes, "until your son or daughter on drugs wants help, no one can help, not even God. I say to anxious parents, 'Be faithful and pray your youngster will be convicted of his need for help. Then, with channels of communication open, when that time comes the youth has a place to turn.' "

Because law enforcement agencies must have citizens' help in locating pushers, Mr. Groen believes parents should be in contact with authorities in efforts to discover sources of supply. One parent's anxiety and concern for others may alleviate heartbreak for a host of others.

Asked how he advises parents faced with the backlash of anxiety which follows a frightening experience with an older child, he suggested parents must keep in mind the uniqueness of each child, each with different temperament, each responding differently to discipline. The young, he said, can see through errors of older brothers and sisters. Often they are more severe in judgment of them than anyone else affected. He reminds parents that their example is stronger than that of siblings.

He says to anxious parents: "Relax. Dedicate yourself to given, specific situations. Have faith in your youth. Give your children to Christ, believing in his power to redeem. Be patient. Don't give up. Concentrate more on spiritual than material needs. Accept God's promise that if you 'train up a child in the way he should go, when he is old he will not depart from it.' And love your child in trouble with a God-like love, even when you're hurting like crazy."

Not every woman knows the anxieties of parenthood, but has a woman lived who has not experienced anxiety and sometimes fear relative to her physical well-being? Doctors would be the first to confirm our fears of physical change, for women by the thousands crowd their offices to whisper, "Doctor, I'm afraid."

Like other anxieties, not all these fears are bad. A recent news article indicates the vast emotional and physiological stress involved in a woman's pregnancy is basis enough for anxiety. In fact, studies show that the expectant mother who hides her anxieties is in trouble. It is a "brittle serenity," one doctor says. The normal woman recognizes her anxiety—about her health, her appearance, her future, her child—and masters it. Openness with the doctor and frank expressions of one's fears is highly important. Women who worry silently, letting their fears eat away into the fiber of their minds, are the ones who give doctors reason to worry.

Fear of disease is actually an anxiety about change. Illness is neither pleasant nor comfortable nor convenient. It is sometimes painful. It changes one's way of life. But while a realistic fear of cancer or some other dread disease may send a woman in for a checkup, an unhealthy fear may keep her from getting a professional evaluation of her symptoms. What she doesn't know may hurt her. The marvelous relief of finding out there is nothing seriously wrong with one's body is, I think, one of the greatest feelings in the world. It is release from anxiety.

Because the transition called menopause is unpredictable, its uncertainties are the basis for anxiety among countless women. Not only is this a time of physical change but of emotional upheaval for some. For biological reasons, a woman who may have achieved a remarkable degree of serenity may suddenly become anxious, suspicious, lethargic, depressed—in short, unserene. Her ups and downs may be as pronounced as those of Jennie, the adolescent next door. Rather than harboring her fears, this is a time for a physician's prognosis and possibly prescription. Suffice it to say here, in our search for serenity, that if she can approach this time of life with facts, rather than old wives' tales; if she can permit herself the luxury of bowing to the demands of these God-given bodies; if she can manage to laugh at herself now and then, knowing she can't completely control the situation, she may get through this time a little more easily.

Not too many years ago the anxiety about approaching old age might have accompanied the menopause. But today most women anticipate a score or more years before they begin to feel old age setting in. We know that old age is not always the most comfortable time of life physically. And it doesn't ease our anxiety one whit to be confronted by those who maintain we should stay youthful looking. "Quick," they say, "with the makeup, the wig, the diet—and here, try this junior-cut dress!" Even though we're repeatedly reminded that the emotionally mature woman grows more beautiful with each passing year. . . .

Longevity brings with it legitimate fears of loneliness, incapacitation, and financial insecurity. The fear of being placed in a nursing home is very real to the woman who has visited friends or relatives in such an institution. It is wise to unmask anxieties about what will happen when one can no longer care for herself. An aging woman deserves to be reassured by her family of their love, concern, and care when she can no longer live alone.

Death is another transition causing great anxiety in some persons. But here again we have a life process to be expected by each of us. A wholesome view of death as a natural event can do much to allay our fears. Certainly a personal and practical belief in eternal life and the resurrection of the dead in Christ to a more glorious life than can be imagined does much to reduce such fears. A physician who deals daily with people frightened at the prospect of death believes that to the extent the fear of dying is described and accepted, to that extent the fear of dying diminishes.

In summarizing a few helps for anxiety over physical change, an accepting attitude of the life processes should go at the top of the list. Then, enjoy the release of expressing your anxieties to your husband, your family, a close friend, or your physician.

Inform yourself what to expect of your body. Let's face it, most of us have some kind of a physical problem at one time or another, and some of us have to learn how to live with a symptom or two. But listen to the body's warning signals and call your physician if they seem significant.

Beware of home medical encyclopedias or a preoccupation with medical articles in popular magazines. Tame that imagination; don't let it run wild.

Look ahead optimistically. Plan ahead sensibly. Hope for the best, prepare for the worst, and relax.

Count on God's grace (he gives it as needed), and let him be your refuge, his everlasting arms your security, in times of physical change.

It is no sin to be anxious. God has built some fear and a certain amount of anxiety into man to prevent a thousand disasters.

But it is over-anxiety of which we must beware. Worry that keeps us constantly upset and torn apart, in a state of mental agitation, is harmful. This is anxiety which has moved into what I consider the "sin" category. And it is something we ourselves can control and cure.

After all, getting down to the benefits of worry, you have to admit it has mighty little to offer. It just doesn't get the job done! "Worry never climbed a hill . . . paid a bill . . . dried a tear . . . calmed a fear . . . darned a heel . . . cooked a meal. . . . Worry never done a thing you'd think it oughta."

It's been estimated that a good 40 percent of the things most people worry about are things that never happen. But, if you're an habitual worrier, let me share with you J. R. Grant's directions which I've kept close by for years:

How To Worry Scientifically

1. Never worry in the dark—get the facts.
2. Decide just what you are worrying about. Decide it definitely and reduce it to a simple statement which you can write down.
3. Worry about only one thing at a time.
4. Set a definite day, afternoon, or night for worrying.
5. Select an air-conditioned room. Lean back in an easy chair.
6. Never worry in bed. That is the place to sleep.
7. Set a time limit to your worrying—say, an hour or two hours—and don't do anything else but worry. Make a thorough job of it during this time.
8. When the time is up, quit. Go to the next problem.
9. Don't worry with a sad face. Smile, sing, whistle!
10. Never worry when you are tired, angry, or depressed.
11. Don't be sorry for yourself.
12. Never worry alone. Take it to the Lord.

While it is possible to overcome worry about many matters, it is impossible to ignore the sincere concerns that sensitive, loving women have for others. As Christians, we have been taught to bear one another's burdens. We cannot help being troubled when we read of the violence all about us, or when our young people make foolish choices, or when illness strikes.

Any wife who suspects infidelity in her husband is going to worry. A mother, seeing her daughter's marriage crumbling, cannot help being troubled. The grandmother of a brain-damaged child—how does one measure that anxiety? A widow whose income won't cover mortgage payments and fixed expenses is bound to worry until she decides what to do about her financial dilemma.

The cares of life are real, and we are constantly faced with new enigmas. But God has made us dependent creatures. He expects us to rely upon him. He waits for us to turn to him. He offers to be loaded down with the burden of our cares, to relieve us of the total responsibility. He says, "Come unto me . . . and I will give you rest."

Next to the reassuring words of our Lord in Matthew 6:19-34 which gave me victory over anxiety during the early hand-to-mouth years of our marriage, I believe Paul's words in Philippians 4 have done most to allay anxiety over the legitimate concerns in my life. The passage has been summed up succinctly: "Worry about nothing, pray over everything, thank God for anything, keep your mind on the right thing."

The entire chapter presents a logical formula for inner peace which includes active concern for others, thought control, personal conduct measuring up to what one knows to be right, and determinedly contented living.

Here is how I like to read it:

"By the help of the Lord always keep up the glad spirit. Let your reasonableness be recognized by everyone. Do not worry about anything, but tell God every detail of your needs in earnest and thankful prayer. And—this is my promise to you if you'll do what I say—the peace of God which transcends all our powers of thought shall guard your hearts and your thoughts in Christ Jesus."

Isn't this serenity?

8
Preparing for Bereavement

". . . those tears will run
. . . in long rivers down the lifted face,
And leave the vision clear for stars and sun."
—Elizabeth Barrett Browning

Loss and death are inevitable. Equally inevitable is the sense of desolation which follows.

All loss is not death. But the loss of any significant love object, be it person, possession, or relationship, which leaves a gap in one's emotional life is bereavement.

A preschooler grieves for her broken dolly. A ten-year-old grieves the loss of her dog. A teen-ager grieves when her romance falls through. Women of every age, uprooted from familiar surroundings, go through a period of grieving. Mothers, left with an empty house as their youngsters move into independent status, experience grief.

Each loss, successfully coped with, prepares us for the deeper loss we suffer when a loved one dies. Yet we are never really ready.

We of the late twentieth century are not so intimate with death. Not often does death occur in the home. Time was when infants died in their mothers' arms. The body of a husband, accidentally killed, was brought home to his wife. Families watched and waited at the bedside of the dying, hearing the last words, hovering close by as the last breath was drawn. The village church bell tolled. The women of the community, sometimes members of the family, prepared the body for burial. The men built the casket and dug the grave. Shops were closed, and everyone attended the funeral. Momentarily, life stood still and tipped its hat respectfully to death. The community mourned and remembered.

Oh, yes, we have seen persons dying on television. Abnormal, spectacular, most often violent death. But we are not often permitted to look upon the shock, the fear, the remorse, the loneliness, the long nights of tears of the bereaved women behind the scenes.

Many families have no experience in mourning other than that in which they participate before their television sets at the death of a national hero. Scattered as they are, they are not often present when relatives, other than the immediate family, have died. Consequently, many come to a time of personal bereavement utterly unprepared.

Because we have been so protected from its realities, many of us have not included death in our philosophy of life. We don't readily accept the fact that physical life is temporary, that we and our loved ones are but transients on the planet earth, here today and gone tomorrow.

Yet death is God-ordained. It was not a part of his original plan, you'll remember, but came upon us because of man's disobedience. And it remains, a reminder of an omnipotent God. A constant reminder that we do not control our destiny. An acknowledgment of death gives us a heightened sense of awareness of the marvelous gift of life.

"Life itself is the greatest miracle!" wrote a dedicated Christian facing an early death from incurable cancer. "My perspective of life is strangely different now. Prior to the onset of this illness my continual thanksgiving to God was largely ritualistic. Now, when I thank him for each new day, it comes from the innermost part of my soul. Each minute that ticks by makes me realize that *all* time is under the administration of God." This man, Albert M. Casteel, forced to include death in his thinking, discovered a new dimension to life.

We who are in search of a lasting serenity need to develop a philosophy of life which includes death. It is not only preparation for dying and for the loss of loved ones, it is preparation for living as well.

Likewise, we must acknowledge the reality of grief. Catherine Marshall expressed its reality succinctly in *To Live Again*: "Grief is a real wound, a mutilation, a gaping hole in the human spirit."

Grief is as real an experience as major surgery. But unhappily, society provides no recovery room where the wounded one is tenderly and patiently watched over until she is ready to move progressively back to normalcy.

The suffering accompanying grief is universal, and in some way or other, "grief work" must take place if there is to be healing of the wounded spirit. Knowing what constitutes healthful grief work gives us a kind of permission to grieve without a sense of guilt, shame, or uncertainty. There is a degree of serenity in the knowledge that a loss of composure is normal.

"It is no sin to grieve," says professional counselor Lofton Hudson. "In fact, it is a sign that the griever is the kind of person who knew how to attach and to care for people." He points out, though, that abnormal grieving may be a sign of immaturity and narcissism, of excessive self-pity or an inability to let go of the familiar and to adjust to present realities.

Certain "normal" reactions emerge repeatedly in grievers, though without any definite order. Of course, the way death occurs affects the way the grief process develops and progresses. Strange deaths tend to create abnormal reactions, and the bereaved in these cases frequently need the services of a skilled counselor.

But typically, initial reactions are shock, confusion, panic, dismay. The death of a loved one is an emotional blow, numbing the senses like an anesthesia. Denial is common in the beginning—"I can't believe it's true. . . ." "Oh, no! Not us!"

There are physical reactions—loss of appetite, dulling of perception, weakness. Grief hurts, often with a tightness in the chest and throat or a feeling of emptiness. We say "the heart is broken." Insomnia is common. All kinds of unusual physical reactions are possible, frequently resembling symptoms which the deceased may have experienced. Nor are these reactions necessarily short-lived. The grief-stricken woman is advised to put herself under her doctor's care and to watch her health, for the body is definitely affected by the deep emotional experience through which she is going.

Another reaction is fear. It is fearful to be in any situation over which one has no control. The very finality of death is fearful. If the deceased was the breadwinner of the family and if the woman has been highly dependent upon him, the fears are understandably increased. Plans for the future may have to be drastically changed, involving a totally new way of life. A sense of foreboding is often experienced.

Then, there is the remorse, the guilt, the self-blame. While not many suffer the extremes of these emotions as do those who may feel in some way responsible for the death, one counselor says guilt is *always* present. If a long illness has preceded the death, one wonders if she chose the right physician. Or if she visited the hospital often enough. If senility and physical incapacitation has preceded the death of a parent or husband, one wonders whether she did wrong in placing the patient in a nursing home. If there was a heart attack, one may wonder why she didn't notice the symptoms of fatigue and restlessness and why she didn't do something to prevent the attack. Or why she hadn't stopped whatever she was doing and given more attention to the loved one. *Why* she hadn't cooked the T-bone steaks he so dearly loved instead of freezing them. Why she had vetoed his idea for a vacation trip last summer. Why, why, why?

If unresolved problems existed between the two prior to death, one is left feeling guilty and remorseful and uncertain about these. There may be bitter memories, the blame for which may have been tossed back and forth repeatedly. Now the bereaved is left with the blame. Little wonder grieving persons are sometimes highly irritable.

To hash and rehash the things which cannot be changed is no solution. These need to be talked out with a trusted friend before being laid aside forever. If there was hostility in the relationship, it may be necessary to seek a professional counselor. Mothers particularly should watch for the problem of hidden guilt in the lives of bereaved youngsters, lest these feelings remain unresolved and result in long-lasting ill effects. When self-blame is justified, the bereaved must keep in mind that what the dead cannot forgive in us, God can. Then she must accept that pardon and cleansing as an accomplished fact, forgiving herself as well.

The emotion of anger is closely related to grief. This may find its object in the most unlikely persons—the doctor or nurses, the minister, the funeral director. Sometimes members of the family turn on one another. God is quite accustomed to being blamed and railed at by the grieving, even by believers: "Why did you have to let this

happen? You should have done something, God!" Even the deceased
may take a lashing: "Why did he have to go and leave me alone with
all these problems! If only he'd taken care of himself. . . . He
wouldn't listen. . . . I *tried* to tell him. . . ."

The desire to be alone is characteristic of the grieving. Some women
say they have ambivalent feelings about solitude. They want to be left
alone, yet they dread it. They want companionship, yet they don't
want to talk. A sense of loneliness, even in the presence of friends and
loved ones, is inevitable.

Those who have studied the grief experience say three things are
absolutely essential to the healthful handling of sorrow. Let me sum
them up simply as *tears, talk,* and *time.*

A friend shared with me something of her agony at the loss of a
precious two-and-a-half-year-old daughter. The mother had been
driving with the child in a sandstorm when the car hit twelve inches
of sand and overturned. The baby was killed instantly. My friend was
hospitalized for six weeks with a broken pelvis. A nurse, she had been
trained to bear up under the tragedies of life with which she dealt in
her profession. So now in this time of personal tragedy she felt she
must be brave. The hospital personnel, she reasoned, were counting
on her. Her family, too—she must act strong for their sake.

But worse than the broken bone from which she suffered, was her
broken heart. Only drugs could ease the pain, and she was becoming
increasingly dependent upon them. Finally, her wise physician, knowing her heartbreak, sat down with her and explained what her pent-up
emotions were doing to her and how the drugs were deterring a
necessary process—that of weeping. She understood, he changed the
dosage, and she wept for three days.

Those who have seen what bottled-up grief can do to people tell
us to go ahead and cry. A stoic hiding of our feelings is not suggested
in the teachings of the Bible. Rather, we read of our Lord's weeping
openly in the presence of both the family and the men who were with
him at the death of Lazarus. We hear him giving his blessing to those
who mourn, "for they shall be comforted." The Scriptures teach us
to "weep with those who weep." And yet we Christians are often

guilty of praising those who "are holding up so beautifully," even
when we suspect they are under sedation, leaving the impression with
one another that not to weep is most commendable.

Unexpressed grief is actually destructive. Therefore, tears shouldn't
be shushed away, for, as a little boy said when told to stop crying,
"Well, what's crying for?" Widows tell us we may expect long sieges
of weeping, sometimes at night, sometimes in the early morning. The
music of a worship service may bring on the tears, or an unexpected
memory, anything familiar however inconsequential. Counselors say,
let the tears flow.

Tears bring relief and, gradually, healing of the terrible wound left
by the death of one who has been so much a part of us. So we mustn't
be afraid to cry. The psalmist wrote, ". . . weeping may endure for
a night, but joy cometh in the morning." A poet says, "There's no
serenity so fair as that just established in a tearful eye."

Not only must there be tears, there must be talk. The deep feelings
of the sorrowing heart must be expressed, if grief is handled health-
fully. For feelings denied expression tend to sap the energy, to distort
reality, to get in the way of healing. An outpouring is so vital and
especially in cases of strange deaths such as suicides. There is need
to tell the story over and over again. Sympathetic and understanding
friends tend to listen kindly to the bereaved as they reminisce. The
good memories tend to completely overshadow the bad, but the
griever needs someone to whom she can express her negative feelings
also, even those feelings of guilt and anger which she would prefer
to hide.

Tears, and talk—and *time*. Grief work cannot be hurried through.
The time it takes varies, of course, depending upon the person and
the depth of the relationship which has been broken. And there is no
definite point when one can say it is finished. For grief may erupt
anytime. Dr. Charles P. Carlson, who shared with me results of his
extensive study on the subject, points out that the wound is often
reopened on special occasions, on birthdays and anniversaries, at the
graduation of a son, the wedding of a daughter, or when some dream
of accomplishment becomes reality. One thinks, "Oh, how proud he

would have been could he have lived to see. . . ." Sometimes, Dr. Carlson says, the anniversary reaction takes place years removed from the loss. Nor is the reaction always quickly dispensed with, for the reopened wound may take some time in healing again.

Someone has said the only cure for grief is to grieve. So if and when grief comes upon us—and it most likely will—we mustn't be like the ill woman who chafes at her condition and makes herself worse in so doing. The time for weeping is not a time for being too severe with ourselves, too determined to keep a stiff upper lip, too self-controlled to give vent to the emotions that are eating away at our very soul. It is a time for self-understanding, for kindness to ourselves. It is a time when we must be very patient, even as we must be following major surgery.

But isn't there anything a woman can do which will help her to prepare for the eventuality of bereavement? We homemakers are great believers in preparedness. We like to have a few groceries on our emergency shelf and clean linens in the closet for emergencies. We believe in the preventive measures of sufficient rest, adequate diet, cleanliness, fresh air, and exercise for the maintenance of good health. Are there not resources which will stand us in good stead when death strikes close by?

Asking myself this question, I came up with five possibilities. I believe we will be better prepared if we will
- make our own memories
- consider saying good-by if there is time
- develop meaningful interests and quality relationships beyond our family
- feed our faith, and
- anticipate recovery.

"God has given us memories that we may have roses in December," James Barrie said. In giving us memories, God has not left us comfortless. For pleasant, loving memories are something no man can take from us. Love is not lessened by loss, and with happy memories I believe it deepens.

A widow whose husband met an untimely death said: "But those were such wonderful years, brief as they were. I wouldn't take anything for my memories." She had not allowed her mind to dwell upon the unhappy moments which occurred now and then in their relationship.

We may have an abundance of those "roses in December" if we concern ourselves with making good memories, *while we may.* Now is the time to begin living with our loved ones so we will have a maximum of joyous recollections and a minimum of regrets when they are gone.

Certainly living to make life easier and more pleasant for those we love would be indicated as a healthful, happy way to live—a way to serenity. But consider the serenity it produces after it is too late to participate in a particular relationship.

Of course, this does not mean living with a total absence of conflict. I doubt if any two people ever thought and felt exactly alike, or pleased each other completely at all times. It is the unresolved conflicts which leave one with regrets and remorse and self-blame in grief.

For this reason, a chaplain said to me, it is wise to live with as much openness as possible in the marriage relationship. For, he said: "The things we feel guilty of later on are those which have remained hidden and unspoken. If a man and woman can hash out their differences and become reconciled to them as they arise, there need be no remorse. We need to deal with regrets while they are fresh, as they come up. Otherwise, they go sour inside and it becomes harder and harder to bring them out into the open where they can be seen for what they are and dealt with accordingly."

The Lord tried to teach this lesson in forgiveness and reconciliation. The spirit of forgiving and seeking forgiveness is the very essence of Christianity. The daily making-things-right-with-others leaves one with the conscience clear and the memory slate cleared of negative recollections.

We have a duty in remembering. Jesus commanded us to remember, "This do in remembrance of me." To remember enhances love and devotion. It does away with a callous taking for granted of our beloved ones who precede us in death.

"The funeral celebrates memory," says Robert H. Bolton, "and memory frees us from time. It can jump over years and call back experiences in the flash of a thought. . . . Memories, the painfully sad and the painfully glad ones, should not be bypassed. Nor should we wallow in our memories or surrender to them, trying to live our whole life in the past. Memory will enrich our lives as we live in the present and move toward the future."

Mr. Bolton suggests that "the memorial service is a channel of God's comfort, hope, and strength to the bereaved. It is an offering of all our attitudes and feelings to God. It is a reminder of our responsibility to one another. It makes us aware of our own mortality.

"The funeral," he says, "provides a stimulus to evaluate one's own goals and loyalties and to dedicate himself to those abiding values which death cannot destroy."

Persons who have arrived at a satisfactory philosophy about funerals prior to the death of a loved one are much better prepared to celebrate the memory of that one effectively. It is extremely difficult to make decisions under stress of bereavement, and families who freely discuss the alternatives before the situation arises are relieved of additional emotional strain, and, often, unpleasantness. Christians should face the alternatives about funerals realistically, if this time of farewell is to be most therapeutic and healing.

For many, there is not time for a farewell to the dying. But where it is possible, the satisfying, though painful, good-by to which response may be felt may be highly desirable, both for the patient and the family. Chaplain Jack Slaughter of the Fort Logan Mental Health Center in Denver feels that, when death is imminent, good-bys should be expressed. So often, he says, the dying, who themselves are mourning the loss of body, family, friends, work, indeed life itself, are deserted by their already grieving families. It is common knowledge among cancer patients that they can know when death is near by the way in which visits decrease and medicine increases. One wrote,

> To die is such a lonely thing,
> We cannot take one friend along:
> To hold a hand would make it
> Far less a frightening song.

Dr. Janice Norton has drawn the picture of the problem of the last relationships with a dying person with great sensitivity in describing her work with a thirty-two-year-old woman. A deep void had been left in this young woman's life by a grieving husband who increasingly busied himself with his work because he could not bear to watch his wife die, by parents who stayed away lest they cry in her presence, by doctors who had become "hearty and hollow" in their frustration at being unable to do anything more.

Dr. Norton wrote: "Mrs. B. was an appealing, attractive woman, warm, intelligent, well read, interested in many things, and capable of very intense feeling. One result of this was that all who loved her and might have been expected to help her with her feelings about dying were intensely and understandably involved in grieving. . . . The very fact of her prospective death had seriously disturbed her relationships with those who meant most to her but had in no way impaired her need for people, had in fact increased it."

The doctor tried to supply the friendship and comfort and understanding so lacking. As time grew short, there was a kind of farewell between the two. The young woman thanked the doctor for helping her, expressed regrets they had not known each other longer, wished they might have had more time together. "She asked me if after her death I would wear for her a red dress she had bought just before she became too sick to have any fun—she wanted 'the dress to have some fun.'" The patient asked Dr. Norton to read Psalm 23. "She said she would miss me terribly but somehow knew I was 'always there' and asked that I hold her hand while she fell asleep."

The psychiatrist concludes that the despair and grief of this woman is far from unusual in dying persons. I share this story with you because the qualities of the relationship which she points out as highly essential in providing comfort to the dying are ones which most women could provide in the event of an extended terminal illness of a loved one. Those qualities are constant availability, reliability, empathy, reassurance, and an ability to respond appropriately to the patient's need—whether to smooth the bed, or feed him, to talk or read, or just sit quietly by. When a woman has given herself to her loved one's need for someone with whom to share the experience of dying, it would seem the days of grief would be sweetened by that sharing.

Chaplain Slaughter said another resource we can store up against the days of grief is in a number of meaningful and quality relationships with persons beyond our family. "Women who have allowed their spouse to be their all in all are in trouble. They've 'put all their eggs in one basket.' The griever will have need to tell the story repeatedly, to people other than the minister and physician, thus the value of friends they can trust and confide in."

A widow, bereaved for some four months, confirmed the truth of his statement. "When one's world is one's family, the loss is worse. For children must grow up and away, and husbands so often precede us in death. If I hadn't been active in church, I don't know what I'd have done. It's late to begin thinking about getting involved after your husband is gone. Then, you've become set in your ways. And in a state of grief and loss, it is difficult to suddenly decide to 'get involved.' "

A teacher said her involvement with her pupils was the saving factor in her bereavement. "I didn't know if I could do it the first day back at school. But my first-graders have done more than anything else to restore me."

Near this teacher lives a childless woman who has no independent interests beyond her home, her husband, and her aging parents. One wonders what will become of her when she is widowed.

The woman with children may think, "Well, I'll always have the children." But she may find herself feeling abandoned and resentful, when soon after her bereavement, they have to leave her to go on about their business of living. And so many families are scattered these days.

Clarissa Start in her perceptive book, *When You're a Widow,* said, "As I analyzed the sorrow of other widows, it seemed to me it was

longest-lasting among those who had little or no creative or humani-
tarian outlet."

One widow suggests a woman needs not just any kind of work, but
work involving people. Another said, "It helps if you have had experience working with the public."

The woman who has denied herself the relationships to be found
in the small-group fellowships of the church may find herself rankling
at the seeming neglect of the church at her time of crisis. Just the
minister's help at this time is not nearly enough. While church members sometimes find in the crisis an opportunity to become friends,
sometimes they leave the grieving one to her own devices because they
find no welcome into her life.

The most vital resource for bereavement, of course, is our faith in
God, and we need to feed it. Nothing is more detrimental than hope-
lessness. And hope is what Christianity is all about. "Bereavement,"
someone has noted, "is the sharpest challenge to our trust in God."

A couple of years ago, at Christmas time, I looked upon the beautiful quality of trust in the faces of an elderly couple who had flown
here for a family reunion, just prior to the departure of a daughter
and her husband for an overseas mission post. While they were enroute from the airport, the word came of the accidental death of the
missionary couple on the highway. Arriving gaily from the airport
in anticipation of a joyous holiday with their loved ones, this father
and mother were met with the sad news. But in the days that followed,
friends who came and went saw a serenity in the faces of those parents
sitting beside each other on the couch. They did not grieve as those
who have no hope. Theirs was a hope born of the trust which characterized their faith in God, a trust fed through dozens of years by their
warm relationship to him and his people.

I saw this same quality of trust in the life of my friend whose little
daughter died in the sandstorm accident. "My child is very much a
part of me. She is a reality in our family. I so strongly believe in the
resurrection. There is no need to go to the graveside." This friend,
with a seriously ill husband, says, "As you know, Martha, I live under
the shadow of death today. But God has given me resources upon

which to draw." She, too, has nurtured her faith in the God who cares and comforts.

One who has not lost a loved one may not be able to fully appreciate the deep meaning of a sermon or a song about the glorious resurrection of our Lord. But the time comes when it takes on new meaning. Someone has said that Jesus Christ went through the grave and left a light burning. That is the light by which we can see as we walk through the valley of the shadow of death.

Even persons who have not made a commitment to God through Christ and those who have been negligent in carrying out their commitment seem to reach instinctively for him in the crisis of bereavement. It is a time when one is more conscious of God. Though there may be moments of hostility, even prayerlessness, yet the overriding emotion will be one of dependency and reliance upon an unchanging God—the same yesterday, today, forever. There is great comfort in the knowledge that Jesus included in his expressed mission on earth the healing of the brokenhearted. His words to the sorrowing, his victory over the grave, his promise of the Comforter cannot be compared with human resources available to the grief-stricken.

Finally, in preparing for bereavement, let us anticipate recovery. Few patients, facing major surgery, expect to die. Admittedly, in the critical days that follow many say they wish they could. But actually they expect to recover.

Likewise, in the long months of suffering following a severe loss, there will be times when one will feel like crying out, "Oh, why can't I die too?" The suffering will seem interminable, but "the night is not forever." Even when more than one loss occurs, recovery comes. I'm thinking of two mothers, each of whom watched two of their children, grown to young adulthood, visibly dying, victims of dread diseases. Neither are the same women they were before it happened, but they have recovered and they have a quality of compassion and tenderness about them some of the rest of us lack.

In an unprecedented way, the indomitable Rose Kennedy has demonstrated to the women of the world that recovery is possible. Seeing her, we wonder how she could bear her losses—two sons, one the recipient of his nation's highest honor, to assassins' bullets, and another son and a daughter in plane crashes, and her husband following long years of incapacitation. In a *Life* magazine interview, Mrs. Kennedy said: "Either you survive or you succumb. If you survive, you profit by the experience. You understand the tragedies of other peoples' lives. You're more sympathetic and a broader person."

Adding, "I made up my mind I wouldn't allow it to conquer me," she expressed the determination, the act of will, necessary for recovery. She does not say she did not grieve, but with each loss (and we're told one loss makes succeeding ones more difficult to bear) she has taken herself in hand, looked about to her family and others, and made an effort to be helpful. "It helps other members of my family if I am cheerful rather than if I were depressed or felt completely beaten," she said.

Certainly her strong reliance upon God has been an asset. Thousands of years ago, a man after God's own heart, David, lost a child. But, relying upon God, he too made a comeback from his grief. Becoming reconciled to the finality of death, he "arose from the earth, and washed and anointed himself, and changed his apparel, and came into the house of the Lord, and worshipped." To his servants, marvelling at his recovery, he said, "Can I bring him back again? I shall go to him, but he shall not return to me." And, the Scriptures tell us, David comforted his wife.

David's hope in the Lord was extremely practical. Not only did he have an assurance that his loved one was with God but also that God was with him. Additionally, he expressed his belief in a future reunion with his child. Such is the comfort and the curative effect of trust in the Lord in times of desolation.

Widows feel highly frustrated trying to find a way of mourning. Some are defeated by lack of direction, others become resigned and passive. Still others become bitter. And others defiant. Widows in other cultures and in preceding generations of our own culture have been far more protected by custom than those today. In our society women are left to their own devices in working their way through the difficult days following the funeral. What they go through, however, is a deeply painful and emotional experience.

Recovery is not only possible, it is probable. Look about you and take note, while you are "whole," of the women who've worked through their grief and today live creatively, even enthusiastically. Most bereaved persons survive their grief and eventually, as Catherine Marshall puts it, begin "to live again."

It's true, we're never really ready. But if our philosophy of life includes death, if we understand and accept grief as normal and necessary, and if we prepare for the crisis through positive, creative living, surely we will regain our serenity.

If You Are Sometimes Lonely

"LORD
The lonely,
Today I feel the quiet despair of loneliness
  throughout the land—
throughout the world. . .
Do not let me rest until I have written those
to whom I cannot go . . . ."
—Antonina Canzoneri

"Please don't leave out loneliness! So many of us are widows," a librarian said to me while "A Woman's Search for Serenity" was still a mere embryo of an idea.

A teacher of creative writing confirmed: "Oh, yes, loneliness is real. I often have my classes write a paragraph on 'My Loneliest Moment' and I've actually wept at some of the things they've revealed."

Our church day care director pictured the loneliness of estrangement. A young man, divorced from his wife and living in another city, came by the church to visit his young son. "He couldn't take his eyes off that child," she said. "And the little fellow wouldn't even look at his father for ever so long. Talk about loneliness!"

Vera, new in our city, offered a favorite family saying on the subject. Soon after one of their many moves, when her husband was out of town on business, she and young Mark were silently munching their supper sandwiches when the boy looked up wistfully at her and asked, "Mom, would you say we're lonely?"

A single woman admitted to her loneliness—"at times, especially when I'm ill." Others, young professionals engaged in church-related careers, commented on their difficulty in finding friends their own age.

A missionary nurse revealed the initial loneliness of retirement. "It's bewildering to suddenly realize you can no longer respond as before to the pleas for medical help in needy areas." And mothers, being retired from active duty by children impatiently claiming their independence, expressed similar feelings at discovering they were no longer needed in the usual ways.

Still other women reminded me, "You don't have to be single, nor in some faraway place, nor an empty-nester, to feel alone." Many of these were women who obviously have everything a woman could desire, but who gain little emotional support from their husbands and enjoy little or no companionship with their families.

Reaching back into the recesses of personal experience, I recalled the lonely times of my life: the loneliness of the young lover's quarrel; of separation from my husband during wartime; of long years when classes, study, and part-time work claimed most of his waking hours; the unique loneliness of the young minister's wife. And my most lonely moment stood out starkly among them all—that day, early in our marriage, when I suddenly realized I was an outsider to that "fellowship of kindred minds" that Christians enjoy. The supreme loneliness, I believe, is knowing one is "outside of Christ," separated from God.

Then I discovered a brand-new loneliness among the multitudes of nonbelievers, my associates in the business world. Polarization takes place, I found, when a believer declares herself. It's a fact— "light hath not fellowship with darkness." It can be lonely out there in the midst of spiritual darkness. The presence of people is no sure guarantee against loneliness.

Studying the effects of urbanization upon drug and alcohol dependency, I discovered that loneliness knows no economic or cultural barriers. Men, strangers in city crowds, going home to drab, cheerless rooms where nobody awaits their arrival; fragile little ladies, being seated separately at tiny tables in busy downtown department store tearooms; ghetto youths, thinking nobody knows them and nobody cares; handsome women in affluent suburbs and luxury midtown apartments, left to their own often inadequate resources by husbands entrapped in the corporate rat race. So many lonely people, so many of them trying to erase their problems with narcotics and barbiturates.

The problem knows no age limitations. William James has observed that "the greatest source of terror to infancy is solitude." I thought of the loneliness occurring repeatedly during the growing years: of the first day in a new school; of being left out of a game or the gang; of not having a date when all the other girls do; of being misunderstood. Listening to the songs of the young in this generation, I wondered if Anne Frank might not have been correct when she wrote in her *Diary,* "For in its innermost depths, youth is lonelier than old age."

But is youth lonelier? In a letter to the *Los Angeles Times,* an eighty-four-year-old woman wrote:

"I'm so lonely I could die. So alone . . . I cannot write. My hands and fingers pain me, pain me. I see no human beings. My phone never rings.

"I'm so very old, so very lonely. I hear from no one. . . .

"Did you ever feel sure the world ended? I'm the only one on earth. How else can I feel? All alone. See no one. Hear no one talk. Oh, dear God, help me. Am of sound mind. So lonely, very, very much. I don't know what to do. . . ."

With her letter came a dollar bill to pay for a phone call, and six stamps, if someone would write. When a news reporter phoned to ask if he might come to visit, she broke into tears. . . . Would you say she was lonely?

All of us are sometimes lonely. But loneliness is not an inalterable condition of the spirit. Inevitable, yes—but capable of alteration.

To begin with, there must be a recognition of the difference between aloneness and loneliness. "Aloneness" is separation from other persons, whether in actuality or by some circumstances (such as traveling "alone"), or by some action or attitude creating a gulf between individuals (as happens with the "loner").

Aloneness, however, is not necessarily loneliness. Alone in your home as you read these words, you may not feel lonely. In fact, you may be completely serene, thoroughly enjoying your solitude.

If you are alone against your wishes, however, you may feel lonely, desolate, dejected at your lack of companionship.

On the other hand, you may have adapted to a situation over which you have no control, and you are enjoying an evening with a book despite the fact no one is beside you.

Two women can be in almost identical situations; the one may feel lonely, and the other not. Elsie wails: "I'm so lonesome I could cry! After I get Harold off in the morning, I nearly go out of my mind, alone in that house all day!"

Next door, Mae breathes, "It's beautiful—a whole day to myself to do just as I choose!"

The difference between the two? The "infinite variety" of women? Or does Mae feel, with Thoreau: "Why should I be lonely? Is not our planet in the Milky Way?"

Admittedly, it's harder to see the stars these days, but those of us with tendencies to inexplicable loneliness might profit from reading the poets who seem to have a sense of kinship with the universe. Then when we are alone, we can know we are not really alone, for all about us are other creatures and "a great wide wonderful world" created by our God. Many persons who most enjoy solitude seem to be keenly aware of their relationship to the rest of God's creation. These are not necessarily hermits with a hideaway in the mountains. A young teen-ager visiting her widowed grandmother in a little Southern city came home reporting delightedly how "she knows every day lily by name, and she talks to the birds and squirrels in her yard as though they're old friends."

Solitude has been called "the school of genius," and while women, for the most part, are not so interested in becoming geniuses as in making their little corner of the universe a little better place for men to dwell, they would profit from more time in that "school."

But this is a day of too much togetherness and too little solitude for many women. Bruce Barton once said: "It would do the world good if every man in it would compel himself occasionally to be absolutely alone. Most of the world's progress has come out of such loneliness." Anne Lindbergh asserted the same truth as she withdrew and brought to the women of the world her *Gift from the Sea.*

It takes time alone for a woman to know herself and to be comfortable with herself. Jesus Christ indicated that he expects his disciples to have a healthy regard for the self, for he taught, "Love your neighbor as yourself." When a woman reaches the point where she is able to relax and enjoy herself without depending on others for pleasure, her fear of being alone diminishes. Really, the self can be an excellent companion. It has many faces, an interesting "personality." Sometimes it likes to be lazy, at others quite busy. Sometimes it wants to think, at other times, it would rather "do." The self is a wonderful companion, especially when one wants to change the mind or the plans rather suddenly.

Time and a kaleidoscope of passing activities can bury the real self of a woman so easily. I had almost forgotten how utterly fascinated I was as a young girl with words in print and beautifully printed materials, until one day at least two decades later, in response to sincere and earnest prayer, God put me into a position where this intense interest was reawakened. I found a whole new way of life which touched off whatever creativity God had endowed me with, absorbing a nameless loneliness, and converting my aimlessness into productive solitude. Other women may find they too would profit by digging through the layers of activity of passing years to find themselves again. The real interests which could make them vital personalities have been buried beneath the superficialities of busy living. Only as we have some solitude in which to be, to feel, to think and to dream—to find ourselves—can we ever hope to bring to those about us the treasure of our best selves. But many a woman has to strive for the very solitude that throws her sister into a state of misery.

We need solitude just as desperately as do our men who retreat to the golf course, the basement workshop, or behind their newspapers. Just as do our children, who need to grow up enjoying, rather than fearing, aloneness.

So, in our search for serenity, we must strive to strike a happy balance between solitude and companionship. And learning to enjoy aloneness, we can face with equanimity the solitary years when they come.

Then, we can invite God into our lonelier moments. The dear, familiar old hymns remind us of this answer to loneliness: "What a Friend We Have in Jesus," "No, Never Alone," "I Must Tell Jesus," and many others. And in a more popular vein, "You'll Never Walk Alone," brings similar assurance.

The psalmist knew the companionship of God in solitude. He was sensitive to God's creation, "When I consider thy heavens, the moon, and the stars"; and to the person of God himself, "The Lord is my shepherd" (with me, beside me, watching over me).

Our Savior's stay on earth was a lonely one. But through his loneliness in crowds, in prayer, on the cross, we catch repeated glimpses of his relationship with the Father. Therefore, the writer of Hebrews suggests, we can rejoice, knowing that our Lord understands our every emotion, including loneliness, and we can openly share with him because he understands.

An awareness of the presence of God and our communion with him in prayer can sustain us in the loneliness of decision-making, a process which cannot always be shared with any other. The knowledge of his presence can reinforce our determination to be true when we find ourselves surrounded by unbelievers and when we are alone with temptation.

Single women may find comfort in the Word of God. "The fact that Jesus himself found it possible and preferable to live and do his work for the salvation of humanity as a single person is significant. . . . It is the privilege of the single adult to identify with him in his singleness," says Evelyn King Mumaw in her little book, *Woman Alone*. She explores the question, "Can Christ really satisfy the un-married woman?" and her conclusions would apply to widow, divor-cee, and the Christian woman out of fellowship with her husband as well. She reminds us that women, regardless of spiritual condition or marital status, have many needs and drives—hunger, thirst, sex, the need for rest, companionship, love, achievement; and so on, but that the deepest needs are spiritual—

The need for forgiveness
    for freedom from guilt
    for assurance of salvation

of hope for time and eternity
for a sense of meaning in life
for purpose in the scheme of things
for motivation with eternal meanings
for fellowship with the Divine.

Christ can satisfy these deepest needs and longings of the soul of a woman, she asserts. While the normal hungers, drives, and human needs are not eradicated by Christ's presence, his presence in the life *puts them into perspective.* In every generation a multitude of Christians, deprived of basic human needs, have attested to this truth.

The very apartness from close human companionship dissipating the potential of some individuals has been the circumstance which has drawn countless men and women into an enviable relationship with the Master. God through his Holy Spirit is able to enter that loneliest of all "lonely's"—the human heart.

Find companionship in a common cause. Look about you at your present relationships. It is possible, with a perfect setup for companionship, to find yourself lonely. You are married and yet you may have lost, or never acquired, a sense of partnership with your mate. Even when you're together, you may feel alone, and lonely.

We have come a long way from the kind of life that required man and wife to work alongside each other in their struggle for survival. With the lessening of shared tasks has come a new problem—a lack of communication.

Catherine expressed the dilemma: "I actually had no idea what Jay did until I visited the company office during an open house." Some women never bother finding out much more about their husband's work than what his take-home pay amounts to. Lovely teen-age girls who prided themselves on following the dating rules of "acting interested" in the major interests and hobbies of their young suitors have often developed into wives who couldn't care less. And they wonder why they're lonely. Others who have carelessly used the information their husbands have shared with them about their work now find themselves outsiders to his business life.

One well-known industrial speaker encourages wives to look upon themselves as partners with their husbands, partners in a profit-making, profit-sharing enterprise. He says all a wife does to make her husband's day more pleasant and his efforts on the job more productive is an investment in a mutual enterprise. She can enjoy a sense of companionship knowing she is a contributing partner, whether it is through setting the mood for a serene, tranquil home, by carrying her load of the discipline of the children, by boosting his morale through constant encouragement (A pat on the back, the psychologists tell us, can help prevent ulcers in our men!), or by keeping herself so well-groomed, mentally alert, and physically fit he'll be proud to introduce her to his associates.

The communication problem within marriage has been rendered complex by the way some corporations have dominated the private affairs of executives, and family life has often suffered at the hands of such a master. A successful corporation wife told me: "I've seen it over and over: men jetting across country away from their families week after week. Sometimes," she said, "they are so exhausted by Friday they dread facing the family problems that have accumulated in their absence and so decide to spend their weekend resting up in some comfortable hotel between engagements."

The emphasis on professional and business advancement as a criterion of success has made "workaholics" of some men, and this has added to the loneliness of their wives. One young professional said, "We knowledge-workers often are so emotionally depleted from our duties when we finally turn to our families that we might as well be absent physically."

A realistic reevaluation of the essentials to a good life is needed in some marriages, and a conscious effort at companionship and mutuality in the partnership may be necessary if communication is to be easy between the two.

Many couples have gravitated to the shoulder-to-shoulder efforts such as their great grandparents might have engaged in, as they have purchased plots of land and have thrown themselves intensely into the building of a second home in the mountains or by the lake. Others have taken to the road with camping equipment, and experienced campers say that camping, without family communication, is a fiasco.

But for many families the companionship is found in an eye-to-eye, heart-to-heart association not requiring such physical effort. It is a matter of the spirit.

One evening at bathtime a little girl took her busy mother's face between her hands and turning it toward her said, "Think about me now, Mommie—nobody but *me!*" Overly busy husbands and wives —and parents—must give some undivided attention to one another, if the gaps of loneliness within families are to be filled. Companionship is more than the physical presence of another human being.

Many otherwise lonely women experience companionship in connection with their work. Depending upon the attitude of a woman toward her job, the hours at work may be very lonely, or they may be highly gratifying. To illustrate: look at two secretaries. One is about as competent as the other, so far as office skills are concerned. But one has only a superficial interest in her job, barriers of distrust exist between her and her supervisor, and a flaunted superiority is evident in her relationships with others in the department. The other has a high degree of interest in the work going on in her office, and there is an easiness of communication between her and her associates. One leads a lonely life at work; the other enjoys companionship in a common cause.

Supervisors often say their jobs are lonely, but even these can be made less so when friendly openness is encouraged in the give-and-take of a team spirit. Often, subordinates are just waiting for a cue to become vitally involved in a common task.

Women who find themselves enmeshed in less than pleasant home and work situations—and admittedly there are many of these in this old world—may find companionship in volunteer work. To have something to do and someone to do it with is so important to happiness for young and old alike. In the chapter on discontent I explored briefly the wide variety of opportunities for volunteer service in communities everywhere. And where there is no ready-made opportunity, there are innumerable needs just waiting to be met by some enterprising person looking for a way out of loneliness. While some women's groups shout, "Down with volunteerism!" let's face it. There's a world of human need which will never be met if an exchange of currency is required. And there will always be people here and there who gain great satisfaction and joy from doing for others, without remuneration!

Someone has said there are but few close personal friends to a lifetime, and volunteer work may compensate in times when there is none close by. The countless men and women with whom I have worked on a variety of projects through the years have provided companionship which has compensated for the loneliness ministers' wives often experience. With them I have shared concern for causes and ideas, more highly gratifying in the long run than the kind of life I might have lived, had I limited myself to an exclusive few special friends.

Society faces a new challenge today: how to provide meaningful activity for the increasing numbers of active, energetic persons reaching retirement age. Dorothy Kostka, "Freedom After Fifty" columnist, notes that retirement communities provide just about everything for their people except opportunities for residents to perform fulfilling and useful roles in society. While she believes it is the responsibility of the individual resident to find his own outlet for service, as in preretirement days, churches and community service organizations can help senior citizens combat loneliness.

In some communities efforts are being made to provide a variety of service opportunities for their more active elders. Employment agencies specializing in placement of retirees are springing up in cities here and there. A "foster grandparent" plan bringing oldsters who love children into contact with youngsters who have no one else has proved highly successful. Churches with day care centers and community weekday programs are meeting two needs simultaneously as they find useful spots where lonely retirees can be put to work in helping others. Some pastors are killing two birds with one stone as they put "people who need people" in touch with one another.

The teacher of a senior class of women in a downtown church is battling the terrible loneliness of some persons in the vicinity of her church by encouraging her "girls" to telephone others who live alone. "In this way they look after each other. Then, when I hear of some ill or shut-in person, I select a member and ask her to call, thus meeting that need, and, just as importantly, giving a Christian woman something to do that assuages her own personal loneliness and her need to be needed."

According to Isabella Taves, author of the column, "Woman Alone," recently widowed women often need the help other widows can provide. She advocates the establishment of widow-to-widow programs under the sponsorship of mental hygiene clinics or family service organizations. One such program, run by widow volunteers in Boston, in three years has provided assistance to over four hundred new under-sixty widows with visits to these women and offers to help in finding new friends, in locating work and in helping children adjust. Companionship comes in sharing a common problem and possible solutions.

And it may come in connection with a hobby! A common interest can make hard and fast friends of utter strangers. Public libraries, YWCA's, adult education classes—all provide a meeting ground for lonely people who have an interest or think they might become interested in a subject. People who otherwise might have no appeal can be very charming when their interest coincides with yours.

Don't be afraid to be friendly. At a morning coffee in our neighborhood one of the old-timers lamented, "Friendliness no longer seems to be stylish. Time was when I visited each new family moving into our area and could always count on a cordial reception. Now when I knock on a door to welcome newcomers, often I'm not invited in." People hesitate, and loneliness spreads. Indeed, in the midst of a population explosion we must restrict the number of persons to whom we relate personally, but sometimes we carry it too far, and we wonder why we are lonely.

The writer of Proverbs set down a classic truth about friendship, "A man that hath friends must show himself friendly." When we withhold ourselves from others, we destroy the very essence of friendship. There must be giving and an accepting response. Some persons have never learned to accept because a bad experience in the past has given birth to distrust. To these lonely ones, friendship cannot be bestowed, it can only be offered. In some cases only persistence in the offering will pay off in a mutually rewarding experience. The person who offers friendship and who is repeatedly rejected will not feel rewarded until acceptance comes.

But . . . "Love is impaired by dread, more or less dimly felt by everyone, lest others see through our masks, the masks of repression that have been forced upon us by convention and culture. It is this that leads us to shun intimacy, to maintain friendships on a superficial level, to underestimate and to fail to appreciate others lest they come to appreciate us only too well," writes Karl Menninger.

"Love is impaired by dread. . ." The wall of dread? Don't walls create loneliness—for us and for others as well? Would we agree that "people are lonely because they build walls instead of bridges"? If loneliness is our problem, we need to give others a chance to get to know us. A woman can speak to her neighbor across her backyard fence without ever being truly friendly. She may attend church Sunday after Sunday without ever getting acquainted with other members —and she wonders why her church is unfriendly. Until she goes out of her way to become involved in one of the many small-group fellowships most churches offer, she may never find even the most casual friendship within her church. For, even when church members visit, it is becoming increasingly difficult to find people at home. One can go for days, weeks, and months in some metropolitan areas without seeing a fellow church member in the course of a weekday. The church is as truly a "meeting house" today as in the early years of American history. And Christian hospitality among church members is as great a need today as when members were widely scattered over rural areas, and friendships waited to be renewed over Sunday dinners after church. Sharing a meal or a snack together has a way of drawing lonely persons closer.

Some persons are naturals when it comes to conversation and

friendliness. Others must consciously seek to develop conversational skills which help them to relate to others in a warm, easy, mutually rewarding interchange of thought, feeling and knowledge. A genuine interest in others, coupled with pleasantness and respect for the other person's worthiness and personal accomplishments, however small, go a long way in developing acquaintances and friends.

Don't overlook the companionship of good books. I wonder if people who have developed a taste for reading are ever lonely so long as they have something to read.

Books! *The New Dictionary of Thoughts* says:

"If you approach them, they are not asleep; if you seek them, they do not hide; if you blunder, they do not scold; if you are ignorant, they do not laugh at you."

". . . a garden, an orchard, a storehouse, a party, a company by the way, a counsellor, a multitude of counsellors."

". . . read, and read, and read again, and still find something new, something to please, and something to instruct."

". . . under every variety of circumstances . . . a source of happiness and cheerfulness. . . ."

"They support us under solitude. . . ."

Even after the eyes grow dim, books in large print make reading possible, and for those whose sight is gone, "Talking Books" can fill the life with companionship. Even the handicapped who cannot hold books in the usual way are provided with devices which make reading possible.

But one cannot read all day, and radio and television bring right into the room of the lonely woman a variety of delightful personalities in exotic settings around the world.

If you live alone, bring something living into your life. Cat, canary, dog, parrot, indoor or outdoor garden—here are the answers to loneliness for some. You see, we humans were created with a need for response, and plants, animals, and fowls are capable of response. How gratifying that response can be—whether it is evidenced through a bird's song, a comfortable furry nestling beneath the hand, obedience, or growth, budding, and flowering. Those of us blessed with an abundance of human response need to be careful lest we criticize unfairly the one alone who pours out her devotion upon something of God's lesser creation. Someone has said, "Until I truly loved, I was alone." We need to love, love seeks response—and only the living can respond.

The superintendent of a home for aging persons, in showing us around his new building, pointed out the deep water-resistant window sills in each room. "So many older persons want something living in their rooms—something their very own to care for. The plants in the sun parlors are beautiful, but they do not meet this need," he explained. Through the window he showed us little plots of ground available to those wishing to work outdoors. The spacious rooms, he noted, make it possible for the resident to bring in the familiar portraits and the cherished objects which speak of home and companionship. Institutional spotlessness that assures good health for the body is not neglected but more humane treatment of the elderly makes provision for the spirit, too.

Refuse to equate aging with loneliness. Rather, prepare for the years when inactivity may be inevitable. Insure yourself against loneliness through the cultivation of an openmindedness. Don't allow yourself to become a bore to family and acquaintances. Be yourself, whatever your interests. In two highly contrasting situations recently, I met two elderly women, each in her own way refusing to equate aging with loneliness. One, a spry little Jewess still active in her organization of university women, has only recently taken up a serious study of parliamentary law. Her vitality of interest in a diversity of subjects surprised and inspired me.

A few weeks later, at a rodeo, of all places, a young lady born in 1899 struck up a delightful conversation with two dude ranchers. Yes, she used to ride, she told us; "now I just clap!" Her rich heritage of life on the big Grand Mesa ranch homesteaded by her parents provided her with experiences which continue to make rodeos and cattle auctions and books about cattle rustling at the turn of the century highly exciting fare. If only we all could live so we could enjoy "clapping" when our age demands less activity!

Intellectual growth and emotional aspirations need not to know any time limitations. I read recently of a ninety-six-year-old man who began taking piano instructions (from a seventy-six-year-old instructor, incidentally). Asked why he wanted to learn to play the piano, he said, "I hear there is a great deal of music in heaven, and I want to come prepared."

Make an effort at being adaptable. The woman who refuses to adjust to new situations can be lonely in a crowd. We make outsiders of ourselves when we refuse to be active participants and contributors to the good life. A mentally alert woman living in a residence for senior citizens might be tempted to retreat into a shell of isolation away from the infirmities and senility about her. But, rather, she participates wholeheartedly in the life of the institution, doing what she can to make life more livable for other residents, giving the hard-working staff a boost with her pleasantness and appreciation, making visitors glad to have been there.

The time to develop adaptability is now—when we may not be alone, for we are in the process of becoming the kind of person we'll be during "the lonely years." Creatures of habit, we become better or worse—more so—depending upon our usual reaction and response to life situations.

Learn to enjoy leisure. By the time most women get around to having *time* to do as they please, they have developed a sense of guilt about loafing. Stop and think about those years when you'd have given anything for a little "puttering" time. You deserve to loaf if your life has been a busy one! It's nice not to have to hurry, for a change, nice not to be hemmed in by a lot of demands. So enjoy yourself. Bask in the pleasures of the little things of life you haven't always been able to linger and enjoy.

*   *   *

And finally, *don't fall victim to self-pity.* A minister said, "Remind your lonely readers to get their minds off themselves. I find a good bit of self-pity in the lonely people I visit. Many of them are never satisfied, no matter what others do for them. Sometimes when I visit, they want to know why I haven't been sooner or oftener (forgetting that others, too, need my ministry), or they ask, 'why doesn't anyone else come?' Some spend so much time thinking about themselves and how the world is treating them that they make their own misery, their own loneliness. If they would transfer their concern for themselves to others, how much better off they would be."

Yes, loneliness is very real. But if you are lonely, don't despair. See if there is something you can do about it. You *can* find serenity in spite of it, in the midst of it. And, if you're anything but lonely right now, insure yourself against loneliness in the years ahead.

- Recognize the difference between aloneness and loneliness. Enjoy the time you spend with yourself.
- Invite God into your lonely moments.
- Find companionship in a common cause—in your marriage, at work, in volunteer service, in a hobby, with others in a similar condition.
- Don't be afraid to be friendly.
- Don't overlook the companionship of good books.
- Bring something living into your life.
- Refuse to equate aging with loneliness. Prepare for the years when inactivity may be inevitable.
- Make an effort at being adaptable.
- Learn to enjoy leisure.
- Don't fall victim to self-pity. Turn your attention outward to others.

10
The Heart Is Restless Till . . .

"Thou hast created us for thyself, and our
heart cannot be quieted till it may find
repose in thee."

—Augustine

Standing there before that smilax-covered altar, we would have objected had someone told us something was missing in our lives.

We were an idealistic young couple, he and I, both church members, of different yet similar denominations. From the first evening of our marriage we read from the Bible together. Because his devout grandmother had instilled in him a sense of the value of the Word, he brought the habit of daily devotions to our newly established home. From the very first paycheck we contributed generously to the church.

But, though we didn't know it, something was missing.

He was the first to discover the missing "something." War had put an ocean between us, but he hurriedly wrote to let me know. No mere mention, but line upon line of joy at his newfound relationship with God through Jesus Christ.

Back home with my parents, lonely and sad at our separation, a little fearful at being pregnant with our first child, terribly frightened by the daily news, I eagerly opened the little photocopied, censored V-mail letters with growing concern and uncertainty. For this something he had found had changed my husband. There was a new depth to his personality, and it reached me across the miles through the closely typed lines of those letters. There was a new, consuming interest in his life.

My fears took on another dimension as I gradually realized that the separation between us was more than mountains and ocean. There was a spiritual chasm.

You can imagine my restlessness—the restlessness of physical separation from him, of the late stages of pregnancy, of uncertainty about the future. And another unrest now—would I know this man when he returned? We seemed suddenly to have so little in common.

But there was yet another restlessness, created by the dawning realization that I lacked a genuine relationship with God. This was what started me on my search.

The search involved a close examination of myself, of my understandings as to what being a Christian was all about. It led to questions, even doubts, about the divinity of Jesus Christ. It forced me to an intellectual examination of the accounts of his life in the Gospels. It ended with the realization that the heart does not find itself in God by gracious deeds or mere mental assent.

"For by grace are ye saved through faith, and that not of yourselves; it is the gift of God, not of works, lest any man should boast," my husband wrote.

Grace? Faith?

Could these be the keys which would unlock the mystery that had sent me on the search? In all seriousness I turned to the family dictionary for meanings I'd somehow failed to grasp in years of church attendance.

> *Grace:* an unmerited, undeserved gift; a favor rendered by one who need not do so; divine love and protection freely bestowed upon mankind.
> *Faith:* a confident belief in the truth, value or trustworthiness of a person, idea, or thing; belief that does not rest on logical proof or material evidence; loyalty to a person or thing.

Rereading the quote in the letter, I substituted these meanings for the words—"for by an unmerited, undeserved act on the part of a loving God, I could be saved by a confident belief in the truth, value and trustworthiness of Jesus Christ as my Savior."

That was a eureka moment in my life. On my knees, in silent prayer, I reviewed the sin in my life; I sought God's forgiveness; I believed with my whole being. And the sense of serenity I experienced in the moments and days that followed has been unforgettable. I had come to the place and the Person where true serenity begins.

Though a woman may not know why, her heart is restless, I believe, until she is reunited with God in what we call "salvation," "the new birth." For we are his creatures, made by him and for him. We have been uprooted from him by sin, and only as we are restored to a personal relationship will we do more than merely exist. All else is a fragile serenity, dependent upon outward circumstances.

Finding the supreme serenity requires something of us, of course. It requires a recognition of our sin and of our need for God; it demands a confession of our sin; it requires an expression of our trust in Jesus Christ as our Savior; and it demands a commitment—a pledge of loyalty and devotion—to him as Lord of our lives. The Bible teaches the one way—the only possible way—for reunion with God is through a heart-belief in Jesus Christ, the eternal Son of God.

It is difficult to communicate this divine happening to mortal minds. Our Lord said it was like the wind which, though one cannot see, is positively there.

I think it is like finding the home of your dreams and moving in. . . . Like being homesick and going home. . . . Like being confined by an illness and finally released. . . . Like being a stunted plant, out of its natural environment, suddenly put into the warm earth where it can respond to sunlight and fresh air and rainfall.

And the benefits!

It is the beginning of a "new you."

It is belonging.

It is being loved—and you know you can stand 'most anything so long as you know you're loved.

It is self-respect, a reassurance of your worth.

It is a settled mind, a this-is-it feeling.

It is an ancient set of values suddenly become valuable to you.

It is support which works when nothing else can.

It is a peace of mind defying all human understanding. . . . Booncy Fullam is a flesh-and-blood illustration of this fact. Her husband went to Vietnam as a fighter pilot. On a mission over North Vietnam his plane was hit and he bailed out. An attempted rescue was thwarted by heavy ground fire, and his parachute was last seen hanging in a tree.

Wayne Fullam has been missing in action nearly five years now, and Booncy and their three sons do not know whether he's dead, or alive in some horror of a prison somewhere.

"Every day was hell on earth," Booncy said. "I thought, 'I can't live, not knowing whether he is dead or alive.' Each morning I would wake up and reality would hit me like a bucketful of cold water. After fifteen months I came to the end of my own strength. Inside my heart I knew that if I were a Christian I should be able to find peace of mind. Wasn't that what the Bible taught? But I didn't have it."

Whatever was missing in her life, she needed it desperately. She had grown up in church, couldn't remember a time when she had not believed in God. But at a luncheon as she heard a speaker point out the inadequacy of an intellectual knowledge of Jesus Christ, she realized that was the extent of her relationship to him.

"I knew who Jesus was, just as I knew who George Washington was. But I didn't follow George Washington, and until that day I hadn't followed Jesus Christ."

She recalls sitting in a big purple chair later and saying, "I've just had it with you, God. It says in your Word that all things work together for good. How can anything good come out of this? And now I'm tired, and you have promised peace of mind. I want this abundant life Christians are supposed to have regardless of circumstances. So you just take over."

The next few days she spent a lot of time thinking about the meaning of the word *belief* as used in John 3:16, and she found it didn't mean intellectual assent, but rather *an adherence to, trust, reliance, putting the whole weight on.* After a Bible class in a moment alone with the teacher, she said: "Tell me something: how can I make myself good enough to be a Christian?" And the teacher laughed sweetly and replied, "You can't ever. . . . You need to ask Jesus to come into your life, and he will make you good enough. *You can't ever do it on your own.*"

First thing she knew, Booncy noticed a change in her attitude. She was even able to smile and sing again. Then, with time, and this was more difficult, she was able to commit her beloved husband, dead or alive, into God's keeping and to ask for courage and strength for the outcome.

Two and a half years later Booncy Fullam had the courage, the boldness, and the serenity to be able to give testimony of her trust in the Lord to an audience of thousands at a Billy Graham crusade. Maybe you saw and heard her on the nationwide telecast.

"Jesus Christ is neither dead nor gone. He is alive and he is alive in me. Give him a chance in your life; you won't ever be disappointed."

Becoming a Christian does not automatically mean lasting serenity, however. The conversion experience is but a beginning. Becoming a new Christian is somewhat like being a completely inexperienced girl on a new job. She's landed the job, but she doesn't know all that's expected of her or what to do next.

A good boss sits down with his new employee and discusses the position. He may hand her a job description outlining her duties. He shows her around the office and makes introductions. He doesn't expect her to grasp everything the first day. He knows it will take time for her to get on to her new role, and he is patient.

The comparison is obvious. God waits for us to sit down for a while and let him communicate with us. He communicates through his Word, through worship, through other believers. He doesn't expect us to grasp everything right at first. He is most patient.

The heart of a new believer will be restless and insecure until she learns what God has in mind for her, once she's decided to follow his Son. Beginning to learn, she is amazed at all there is to know. She begins to see herself in a new light, a highly revealing light which magnifies her imperfections. She begins to find out how reliable her God is, and the conditions upon which his generous promises depend. She begins to discover what he expects of her in worship and in service to others. She hears his command to share the news of what has happened in her life. She finds out that *what he really has in mind is for her to become like his Son.*

This last realization—that she is to become like Christ—is the big order.

What we may become with Christ in our lives is spelled out in a thousand ways in the Scriptures. Paul put it this way in Galatians 5:22: "For the fruit of the Spirit is love, joy, peace, longsuffering, gentleness, goodness, faith, meekness, temperance." The translation of "self-control" for the last word is more meaningful to me.

The women of old Trinity Methodist Church in downtown Denver have pictured these qualities in a way particularly appealing to women. At the front of a red-carpeted assembly room they have hung an embroidered picture of a tree on which are nine varieties of fruit. Along the walls, from heavy gold rods are long tasseled hangings in beige canvas and red felt, enlargements of the fruit—one depicting love, another joy and so on. With sequins, pearls, and bits of braid and with exquisite embroidery of gold, silver, and black the women have pictured, as best they could in still life, the beautiful qualities Paul enumerates.

Sitting in that room, I meditated upon the lessons it teaches: The one tree from which all of these fruit are nourished—the Spirit of God within the believer. The embellished hangings, evidence of hour upon hour of painstaking needlework, spoke of time. The missing ones (all were not yet in place)—a reminder that these Christlike qualities do not always appear simultaneously, and seldom overnight.

Surrounded by those brilliant symbols, I experienced a new awareness of the radiant beauty God wants to bring out in us. The fruit of the Spirit are not mere words—to be seen upon a wall or read in a book. They must come to life in people—this is what God has in mind. And the heart is restless until they are actualized in us. For there is little enough serenity where there is ill will, misery, conflict, impatience, harshness, distrust, pride, and lack of restraint.

The personality is the means by which we give expression to the Spirit within us. And great serenity awaits the woman who finds a way of life, especially suited to her, through which she may live the

Spirit of Christ. An artist, an expert on floral arranging, has written, "When we do find a medium that fits our needs—and use it—then into our lives comes fulfilment and a sense of peace." She spoke of an art medium, but the truth applies to modes of expression not classified as art. A part of serenity is being free to find creative ways of expressing Christ-in-us to others.

The woman who has not "found herself" in an involvement which gives her opportunity to be her true self continues to be restless. I believe many continue to grope because of the rapid changes in our culture. But others have found themselves—one, a children's worker in the church; another, at her joyous best helping needy persons; another, a homemaker providing a home away from home for a steady stream of displaced young people; yet another, expressing herself through her career.

As valuable as involvement is to the growth of a Christian, however, it is not what God is most concerned about. He is not nearly so impressed with what we are doing as with what we are becoming. Performing good deeds while yielding to pride, jealousy, and criticism falls far short of what God has in mind. Eloquence, generosity, and sacrifice are nothing, Paul reminds us, unless they are done in love. Being, not doing, is the summum bonum of the Christian life.

God does not expect us to imitate the works of the "best Christian" we know. This would be fatal, particularly if she's an energetic youth worker and we are intimidated by teen-agers; if she's an ardent leader, and we're not the "chief" type; or if she is a soprano, and we're tone deaf. We need not be threatened by others. A schoolteacher, growing in maturity, put it well: "I used to be afraid of what people thought of me. Now I try to maintain a personal relationship with God, seeking his guidance through the Bible and prayer. Now, when I find myself worrying about what people may say, I confess it as a sin and tell God what *he* thinks is most important to me."

The believer who has not begun to express the spirit of Christ, even in the most amateur ways, will be restless. Suppressing the spirit of God within her, she is in conflict. It is the age-old conflict between good and evil. Peace of mind—serenity—means absence of inner conflict. I believe a woman's heart will not be quieted 'til she says "yes" to the Spirit and discovers personal ways of expressing love, gentleness, self-control, and the other qualities of the Spirit.

So often, however, we limit God's working in our lives. Christian growth takes place in proportion to our commitment, our desire to grow, and our willingness to develop. The will is involved in our success as Christians, even as it is in any worthy endeavor.

For instance, Carol, a woman in her late thirties, had always wanted to be a social worker. Recently she enrolled in courses leading to a degree in social work. For years she had felt a commitment to this kind of work; now her desire is strong enough to cause her to invest time and money in preparation, and she is willing to make the mental and physical effort to accomplish her goal. Likewise, a commitment to Christ without a desire to mature and a willingness to change will remain superficial and unfulfilled.

We have to do our part. A plaque in my dentist's office puts it this way: "There is nothing the dentist can do which will overcome what the patient will not do." Now, I would not dare limit God's ability to overcome our stubborn wills, but I am confident there is nothing he will do to overcome what his people refuse to do. He will not override your refusal to try to control your temper. If you insist you are an impatient person and will never be otherwise, he doesn't defy you and make you patient in spite of yourself. If you have ill will toward your mother-in-law and don't care who knows it, nor do you intend to change that attitude, God will not intervene.

Too often we've soothed ourselves by telling each other to "just live close to the Lord" and everything will be fine. It would, if we maintained a warm, continuing relationship in which we were deeply aware of our heavenly Father. But usually we stand around waiting for a miracle to change the negative responses that keep our lives turbulent and unserene. The apostle Peter did not think that was the way to mature as a Christian (and he had a rough experience in growing toward Christlikeness). Recalling that God's divine power has bestowed upon us "everything that makes for life and true religion," he says we should *try our hardest,* really exert ourselves, to supplement our faith with love, moral character, intelligence, self-restraint, endurance, and devotion to God. This is not salvation by works, rather it is the fulfilling of our salvation in active discipleship.

Getting to know Jesus Christ and to love him makes much of the effort a real pleasure. For love has a way of making a privilege out of duty. Growth takes place, and serenity comes, when one makes a spontaneous response to the Spirit within. There is a togetherness in the effort, even as there is when two persons enter into any task with interest and enthusiasm.

Merely going through the motions of living the Christian life, we cheat ourselves and the heart is restless. The most miserable Christians are those who live in defiance to what they know the will of God to be. Others, who give no more than dutiful compliance to his will, wonder where all the joy is.

An office supervisor, commending the enthusiasm and interest of one young woman on her staff, decried the big majority of people who merely go through the motions of their work. "They deny themselves the joy of living by not entering into their daily tasks." It's the old truth that you get out of a thing just about what you put into it. Christians who maintain no more than a casual relationship with their Savior likewise find little satisfaction. Living on the periphery of their churches, putting little or nothing of themselves into the work, they find little fulfilment there. And the world wonders why. Dr. Ernest T. Campbell has said, "When Christians lose the spring in their step or the smile on their face the fault isn't that they are Christians but that they aren't Christian enough."

The striving required of the Christian makes an adventure of living. As F. W. Robertson put it: "True rest is not that of torpor, but that of harmony; it is not refusing the struggle, but conquering it; not resting from duty, but finding rest in it." Indeed, the heart is truly restless when no challenge awaits it.

Finally, I believe the heart is restless until it realizes the Christian life is a "becoming" process. Maybe you've seen the lapel button on which are these puzzling letters: PBPGINFWMY. Every Christian is eligible to wear one—the letters stand for "Please be patient. God is not finished with me yet."

All of us are still in process. Carl Rogers, one of America's most distinguished psychologists, has written a book titled *On Becoming a Person*. He believes it is urgent that persons accept themselves as "a stream of becoming, not a finished product . . . a fluid process, not a fixed and static entity; a flowing river of change, not a block of solid material; a continually changing constellation of potentialities, not a fixed quantity of traits . . . a pliable personality open to improvements and enhancement." There is a world of hope in the thought, especially for one with Christ in the life.

God knows best of all how really "unfinished" we are. He has made us that way, with a lot of growing to do mentally and physically. At the new birth, again we are but "babes in Christ," spiritual infants. But within us from birth is an impulse to grow, and after conversion there is a strange compulsion to live up to his ideals for us. We try—we fail—we try—we fall short—we keep on trying. We wonder why we keep at it, but the challenge of perfection urges us on. To be perfect, we know, is impossible in this world. But a voice insists we keep on becoming. "Be ye perfect, even as your Father which is in heaven is perfect." The promise is clear, "He which hath begun a good work in you will perform it. . . ." The genuine Christian cooperates.

Sometimes becoming is uncomfortable, even painful. It actually takes a lifetime. Like the "magic of real" in Margery Williams' *The Velveteen Rabbit:* "It doesn't happen all at once. You become. It takes a long time. That's why it doesn't often happen to people who break easily, or have sharp edges, or who have to be carefully kept." Sometimes, as the old skin horse tells the little toy rabbit who wants to become Real: "Most of your hair has been loved off, and your eyes drop out and you get loose in the joints and very shabby. But these things don't matter at all, because once you are Real you can't be ugly."

Once a Christian is well along the way to having love, joy and peace, patience, gentleness and goodness, faith, meekness, and self-control in her life, she'll no longer be worrying about how she looks. And people who have learned what's important in life won't see an ugly face, a bulky figure, wrinkles, or graying, thinning hair (if it takes that long). They'll see, instead, a reflection of Jesus Christ.

It is God's love which works the miracle of becoming. Jesus told the twelve, unlikely prospects that they were, "I will make you to become. . . ." He singled out Simon the big fisherman and said, "You're going to become, not shiftless and unreliable, but strong, stalwart, rock-like, dependable." Looking beyond the problems in the life of the woman taken in adultery, he saw what she could become. "Go and sin no more," he encouraged. Knowing the wise and loving person that young son of thunder John would become, he refused to disqualify him.

He knows we're persons in process, not finding all of the peace that passes all understanding in the rush of one great discovery, but rather bit by bit. He promises that one of these days, "when he shall appear, we shall be like him, for we shall see him as he is."

Until then, we must continue in our search for a lasting serenity.

Acknowledgements

Ninki Hart Burger, *The Executive's Wife* (New York: The Macmillan Co., 1968).

Arthur Gordon, "The Engaging Art of Laughing at Yourself," "Getting More out of Life" (Pleasantville: Reader's Digest Association, 1970).

LaVerne Hull, advice on boredom, *Republican-Standard*, Waukon, Iowa. Reprinted in *McCalls*, May 1961. Used by permission.

Mary Ann Hamilton, "Dream a Possible Dream," *Empire*, March 28, 1971. Used by permission.

Ida Nelle Holloway, "It Is with Regret," *People*, March 1971.

Joan Erikson, "Notes on the Life of Eleanor Roosevelt," *The Woman in America*, ed. Robert Jay Lifton (Boston: Houghton Mifflin Co., 1965).

Morton M. Hunt, *Her Infinite Variety: The American Woman as Lover, Mate and Rival* (New York: Harper and Row, 1962).

Peter Drucker, *The Effective Executive* (New York: Harper and Row, 1966).

Rona Jaffe, *The Best of Everything* (New York: Simon and Schuster, 1958).

Duane Valentry, "Don't Be a Crime Victim," *Today's Health*, February 1968.

J. R. Grant, "How to Worry Scientifically." Used by permission.

Albert M. Casteel, "A Christian Facing Death," *Rocky Mountain Baptist*, March 19, 1971.

Robert H. Bolton, "To the Congregation at the Funeral Service," *Church Administration*, April 1971.

Janice Norton, M.D., "Treatment of a Dying Patient," *The Psycho-analytic*

Study of the Child, Vol. 18 (New York: International University Press, 1963).

Antonina Canzoneri, "Contemporary Missions Prayers," *Royal Service,* August 1971. Used by permission.

William Endicott, "Woman of 84: Isn't Anyone Else Lonely," *Los Angeles Times,* November 26, 1970. Used by permission.

Evelyn King Mumaw, *Woman Alone* (Scottdale: Herald Press, 1970).

Karl Menninger, *Love Against Hate* (Harcourt, Brace and Co., Inc., 1942).

The New Dictionary of Thoughts, ed. Edwards, Cantrevas, Edwards and Browns (Standard Book Co., 1966).

Booncy Fullam, "Missing in Vietnam," *Decision,* August 1971. Used by permission.

Carl Rogers, *On Becoming a Person* (Boston: Houghton Mifflin, 1961).

Margery Williams, *The Velveteen Rabbit* (Garden City, Doubleday, CL).

The New English Bible, The New Testament in 26 Translations, and others.